GREAT SKI COUNTRY CONDOMINIUMS OF AMERICA

GREAT SKI COUNTRY CONDOMINIUMS OF AMERICA

Written by Miles Jaffe

Photographed by Maria Hults and Robert Ricke

Introduction by Ernie Blake
Founder, Taos Ski Valley

SKI THE BEST, INC
New York, New York

To Julie who worked so hard on this book,
and finally gave up on us all.
Miles Jaffe

To Lloyd Zeiderman . . . Friend, Mentor,
Confidant . . . without whom much
in our life would not be.
Maria Hults and Robert Ricke

Library of Congress Cataloging-in-Publishing Data

Jaffe, Miles
Hults, Maria, & Ricke, Robert, Photographers
Great Ski Country Condominiums of America

1. Ski Resorts—United States
2. Ski Resorts—Canada
3. Condominium Resort Properties
4. Resort Accommodations

Library of Congress Number: 88-92280

CONTENTS

CONTENTS

Foreword

This is a guide to skiing at 45 of America's principal destination ski resorts and to leading rental condominium properties at those resorts. It is a companion book to **Great Ski Inns and Hotels of America**, published by Ski The Best in 1988.

The condominium is hardly the subject of affection or romance, unlike, for example, the inn. The term itself is unappealing, being legal in origin and having connotations of uncaring development or monotonous, impersonal housing. The term aside – and it is hard to find a more satisfactory one, many of us stay in vacation apartments when we ski. Our hope is that this book will make the choice of condominium accommodations more informed for most of us than it has been in the past.

The condominiums we have chosen are often, but not always, deluxe. Many are the best in a particular resort. Each has a reason to recommend it whether it be for its location, its supporting athletic and vacation facilities, or its suitability for particular groups or people.

In the appendix, we have included details on the condominiums – rental costs, associated facilities, square footages and the telephone numbers of the property management groups from which these apartments can be rented.

Because the subject of condominiums lacks *caché*, few books have attempted to review them. However, their use and their growth do tell us about changes that have taken place in skiing. In the 1960s skiing's popularity soared. Families flocked to this sport, one of the few which members of a family could do together. Just as groomed slopes were added to the rugged trail to meet the requirements of family skiing, so condominiums replaced inns as the most suitable accommodations for groups and families.

In the late 1980's, as visitors to ski resorts sought more balanced vacations involving alternative sports, shopping and relaxing, vacationers, many of whom skied little or not at all, wanted to be in a town, not in the woods. Vacations, on skis or off, need a village center be it Zermatt, Vail, Park City, Manhattan, or Sausalito. Many of the apartments which we review are built in clusters in wooded settings. But many others are village apartments. This book opens and closes with two resorts, Stratton, Vermont and Whistler, British Columbia, which in the 1980s created slopeside pedestrian-only villages. Almost as if to confirm their leadership, in the summer of 1988, these two forward-looking resorts also installed a 10-12 person stand-up gondola, the newest lift technology.

We are pleased to have our Introduction written by Ernie Blake, ski pioneer and founder of Taos Ski Valley. In the Introduction, Ernie puts these recent changes in skiing into the context of the history of skiing. Ernie began skiing in the Alps as a child during World War I, and has skied every winter since then except for three winters during the last World War. In the early 1950s in his own private plane, he searched the southern Rockies to find the site for a new ski area. Taos Ski Valley is now one of America's most prominent and diverse ski resorts.

We thank Ernie Blake for putting the short span of our involvement with skiing into the broad picture of the development of this sport of which he has witnessed so much. The pioneers of the sport, like Ernie, have shaped the rapid changes that have come to skiing. The best, like Ernie, have also slowed the monster of development to preserve what we treasure of the past. The condominium is part of both the progress and of the monster. We have not attempted to deal with this paradox. That is for each of our readers.

Ski The Best publishes a newsletter reviewing ski resorts, travel, accommodations, restaurants and other services connected with skiing. We at Ski The Best are always searching for a match of resort or accommodation to skier. We hope this book will help you find your match.

Miles Jaffe
Ski The Best
80 Eighth Ave
New York, NY 10011

THE SNOWY PATH FROM IGLOOS TO CONDOMINIUMS by Ernie Blake

The use of skis is 5,000 years old. Originally, skis were used, primarily along the northern rim of the Eurasian continent, as a means of transportation over flat or hilly country. Overnight shelter was found in caves or igloos. Petroglyphs found in Sweden and Norway depict skiers hunting big game 4,000 years ago.

The Origins of Alpine Skiing

Skiing as a sport is about 100 years old, though Scandinavian miners were already using skis for downhill competitions in two northeastern counties of California in the 1850s. In Europe, university students, game wardens, foresters and the military became interested in the new sport after the Norwegian scientist and explorer Fridtjof Nansen crossed Greenland on skis with a group of Norwegian savants in 1888.

Sometime between 1898 and 1900, an unknown Norwegian skier adapted sealskins to the running surface of his skis permitting him miraculously to climb uphill. Winter mountaineering came of age and simple high-altitude shelters used by cattle herders in summer when grazing their herds were converted into winter shelters. Skiers slept in the hay, without the luxuries of running water or electricity. Food and wine had to be brought in by each visitor. Early in this century, mountaineering clubs expanded these shelters and the number of skiers grew.

The Ski's Evolution

Skis quickly changed as well. Norwegian skis, 250 to 300 centimeters long, were designed for travel across flat or hilly country. The binding was loose making turning, at best, difficult. In the 1890s, an Austrian mining engineer, Mathias Zdarsky, designed a ski approximately 170 centimeters long with a waist, a narrow middle, which made turning easier and worked in the steep terrain of the Alps. After much experimentation, he devised metal toe irons which gave the skier lateral control. Zdarsky, as his Scandinavian precursors, used only one long pole, but he developed a method of turning somewhat similar to what later was called a "stem turn." With religious fervor and at his own expense, he traveled all over the Alps teaching people his new method.

Another Austrian, Hannes Schneider (1880-1955), modified Zdarsky's snowplow position. Using two poles and sitting way back on his skis, he carved elegant patterns in the vast powder fields of his native Arlberg region of Austria. At age 17, he was invited by the major hotel owner of St. Anton to create the first organized ski school. St. Anton became famous for its ski school and its tourist trade boomed.

As skiing became easier to learn, other summer resorts eagerly added a winter season: St. Moritz, which two thousand years earlier had been a famous hot springs spa for the elite of the Roman Empire; Zermatt, which had been a long-time summer resort favored by the mostly British mountain climbers. Mürren and Grindelwald followed when their British visitors organized skiing and ski competitions for their golden youth.

INTRODUCTION

Hotels were small in most instances and rooms rarely had running water. Maids brought pitchers of water to the rooms, and guests paid a service charge of a Franc or two whenever they permitted themselves the luxury of a bath.

At first the "locals" took little interest in skiing, a sport for crazy Englishmen and college students. Henry Lunn, a British travel agent, promoted a winter season in Mürren reserved for the members of elite British prep schools and universities. In 1910 a British general gave his name and that of his military victory in the distant Afghan city of Kandahar to the first major international downhill competition. Progress in equipment and in teaching methods made skiing into a mass sport in the '20s and '30s. Steel edges came on the scene in 1930 and cable bindings in 1932-33. These bindings permitted forward-leaning, the first step to parallel skiing and also the cause of injuries, until the release binding began to function reliably, twenty years later.

The Ski Resort

Skiing was revolutionized when, in the depths of the terrible economic depression (1931), two resorts built uphill transportation specifically designed for skiers: the Corvigliabahn in St. Moritz and the Parsennbahn in Davos. They were immediate financial successes. The idea of building trams to draw winter tourists to what had been just summer resorts spread like wildfire. These lifts attracted a more affluent and sophisticated group who would never have climbed a peak, but did not mind paying for a fast and smooth ride uphill. These moneyed skiers filled the great hotel palaces, many of which had been standing empty since the crash of October, 1929. Originally created for summer vacationers, these hotels offered luxurious accommodations and superb food, drink and entertainment.

Also in 1931, Signor Agnelli of Fiat automobile fame and fortune, built the first planned super-resort in the vast, as yet uninhabited mountain landscape of northeastern Italy. Sestriere included two circular tower skyscrapers with cable cars emanating right from the hotel lobby. In 1935-36, Averill Harriman and the Union Pacific Railroad developed a similar dream village in the empty sheep grazing lands a mile from Ketchum, Idaho: Sun Valley. Mr. Harriman also had his railroad engineers design the chairlift which has since become the dominant uphill mechanism for skiers all over the world.

Modern Skiing

In 1950, three American technological innovations changed the sport further: Howard Head invented a ski which made deep snow skiing easy, even for duffers; Joe Tropeano found a way to make snow by shooting water and compressed air through snow "cannons;" and Steve Bradley, manager of Winter Park in Colorado, designed the first slope maintenance device, a skier-pulled roller. All three developments made skiing easier and reduced the nagging fear of snowless Christmas vacations.

Since the end of World War II, skiers have moved from the reality of simple hay lofts and spartan dormitories to the expectation of luxurious rooms with attached bathrooms and fireplaces, television, telephones and access to saunas, jacuzzis, squash courts and olympic-sized swimming pools. In the 1960s, the cost of building luxury hotels threatened to slow down the growth of ski resorts. That, in turn, alerted the legal profession, the realtors and the tax experts to create the legal framework for the condominium, where the unit owner owns just his apartment and the plot on which it stands. The idea was a great success because it made owning a home in the mountains initially affordable and eased the option of rental income. It made mountain living a pleasure since the onerous jobs of snow removal from roofs and driveway, the melting of frozen water lines or the acquisition of firewood all became the problem of the condominium manager, rather than the apartment owner. In addition, the cost of saunas, steamrooms, exercise equipment and all marketing of rental units was spread among many owners.

I have watched skiing change over the 71 years in which I have been involved in it. I have seen Taos Ski Valley start from scratch with one log cabin and a T-bar. It is now transformed from a tiny community to one with several inns and many condominiums and private homes. We in Taos, nostalgic for the past, struggle always to accept but to modify the change which has come to the Ski Valley. The condominium now joins the inn as a primary form of ski vacation housing.

Ernie Blake
Ski Pioneer & Founder of Taos Ski Valley
Taos Ski Valley, New Mexico, USA

INTRODUCTION

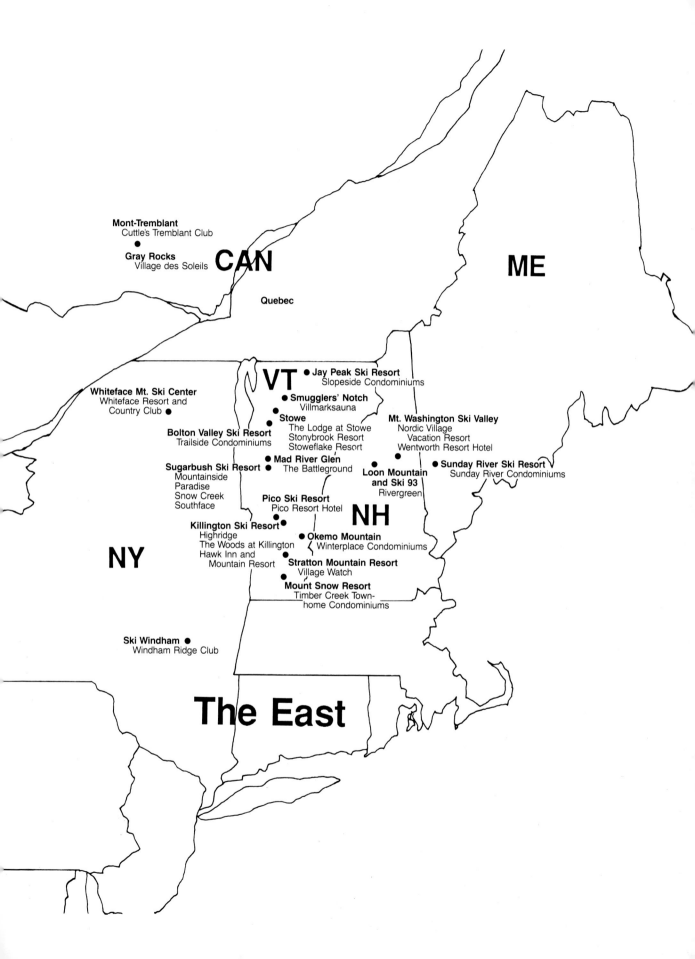

Mont-Tremblant
Cuttle's Tremblant Club ●

CAN

ME

Gray Rocks ●
Village des Soleils

Quebec

VT

Jay Peak Ski Resort ●
Slopeside Condominiums

Whiteface Mt. Ski Center
Whiteface Resort and
Country Club ●

Smugglers' Notch ●
Villmarksauna

Stowe ●
The Lodge at Stowe
Stonybrook Resort
Stoweflake Resort

Mt. Washington Ski Valley
Nordic Village
Vacation Resort
Wentworth Resort Hotel

Bolton Valley Ski Resort ●
Trailside Condominiums

Sugarbush Ski Resort ●
Mountainside
Paradise
Snow Creek
Southface

Mad River Glen ●
The Battleground

Loon Mountain
and Ski 93
Rivergreen

Sunday River Ski Resort ●
Sunday River Condominiums

Pico Ski Resort ●
Pico Resort Hotel

NH

Killington Ski Resort ●
Highridge
The Woods at Killington
Hawk Inn and
Mountain Resort

Okemo Mountain ●
Winterplace Condominiums

NY

Stratton Mountain Resort ●
Village Watch

Mount Snow Resort ●
Timber Creek Town-
home Condominiums

Ski Windham ●
Windham Ridge Club

The East

STRATTON MOUNTAIN

STRATTON, VT

Stratton has matured into a luxurious full-service resort. The new mountain village at the base of the slopes connects the familiar day lodge and clock tower with an abundance of new lift-served vacation housing. The shops, boutiques, and restaurants along the village pedestrian thoroughfare supply the essentials of life as well as the sense of a lively little town. Up on the mountain, trails have been broadened to give something of the open feeling of Western skiing. The lift system has been transformed by the launch of Starship 12, America's first twelve-person stand-up gondola.

The Skiing

The mountain itself, with only one steep drop and a couple of bump runs, is not perilous. The Starship, however, will be the instrument of cruisers' delight. Skiers who are bump-adverse will be able to shoot down 1,750 feet of vertical and fly back up on the seven-minute gondola. We're not sure what this dizzy pace is going to do to the skiing; we do know what its going to do to your legs.

Novices and intermediates will appreciate the broader trails, the expanded snowmaking and the passionate grooming. Beginners will find appropriate terrain toward the bottom of the mountain and novices with some experience and reasonable caution will be able to explore the peripheries off the top.

Resort Life

We can remember when Bondville, down at the foot of the mountain, and Haigs restaurant-discotheque were "at the resort" and Stratton's primary service center was Manchester Center. No longer. The critical mass has shifted to the base of the mountain and its array of essential community components, including restaurants and cafes as well as grocery, furniture, equipment and clothing stores. The new Stratton, with some parking underground already, is on its way to becoming a car-free village. Walking to the Sports Center, 500 yards down the hill, can be counted as an independent exercise, separate from its indoor tennis, racquetball, or exercise classes.

Stratton is an archetype of change in ski resort living. The rugged rustic mountain and the quaint country inn have been supplanted by groomed terrain, guaranteed snow and a luxurious vacation village at the base of the slopes.

Mountain Statistics: Vertical, 2,003 feet; Hourly Uphill Lift Capacity, 18,000 skiers; Skiing Terrain, 400 acres.

VILLAGE WATCH

STRATTON MOUNTAIN, VT

Each successive decade in the history of skiing has provided its own candidate for the accommodation of choice. Once upon a time, the Sun Valley Lodge epitomized fashionable ski vacationing. In the early '60s, Vail popularized the village-from-scratch and introduced skiers to privately-owned apartments called condominiums. New England's country inns flowered in the '70s and '80s, offering cozy nostalgia to a generation of skiers. The grand hotel, the rustic cabin, the boarding house and the roadside motel all have had their skiers in their day. We cheerfully predict that this century will close with the vacation apartment in the on-mountain village as the skiers' accommodation of choice.

Stratton's Village Watch apartments illustrate why. They are like a trampoline, an ideal jumping-off point for any of Stratton's several attractions.

hits of the last several decades from his second floor perch, while tables are moved aside creating a dance floor below. The village now has a social center, the center of life of the entire resort.

A Village Watch apartment is large; large enough for a big family, or for two medium-sized families, or for three or four couples to share. Group intimacy and individual privacy are each promoted architecturally, with a Great Room for socializing and dining, and smaller bedrooms on separate floors. Sharing is not only companionable, it's also economically advantageous.

The apartment on the mountain extends the individual freedom of its residents. Absent group consensus, individuals may sleep late or ski early or lunch at home or change hats or quit after one run or ski until dark. The children are freed from being relentlessly looked after. Parents are freed to pay attention to themselves. The vacation becomes a vacation.

From these apartments, the children can find their own way through the village to Stratton's active children's ski school. The child-care program looks after kids six weeks to three years old, and above three, children join the ski school's Little Cub program. Racing programs start early and by the age of 8, advanced learners can join a racing team. Parents can devote themselves to other pursuits while the kids learn to ski.

Walk out the front door into the little village street with jewelry, furniture, and clothing stores on either side and no cars in the middle. Walk down the street in either direction to ski lifts, wander into a gallery or antique store. Do your business at the bank.

At the heart of the village are the Clock Tower Cafe and Mulligan's. The Cafe serves a light snack menu all day. Mulligan's is a two-story restaurant built in an urban modern Victorian style. Its bar survived San Francisco's earthquake and was transported across the country to be the centerpiece of the lively interior. Above the bar in the late afternoon, the sports event of the day can be seen on television. In the evening, a dee-jay plays

MOUNT SNOW RESORT

WEST DOVER, VT

Mount Snow Ski Resort is the combination of a huge mountain and a long valley with two traditional New England towns. The mountain has modern lift and snowmaking systems, and more skiers than any other downhill area in the East, save Killington. The valley and its villages, West Dover and Wilmington, have distinguished old inns and handsome new condominiums. The combination results in a lively, diverse resort.

The Skiing

The face of the mountain is broad and long, 7,300 feet of incline over a vertical of 1,700. This ratio provides an abundance of good intermediate cruising terrain, with broad novice slopes at the base. The novice terrain was augmented by the incorporation into Mount Snow of neighboring Carinthia. In addition to the broad front is the North Face, which has a vertical of about 1,000 feet and six narrow, steep expert trails (including Jaws of Death and P.D.F.), the most challenging skiing south of Killington. Mount Snow, a part of SKI Corp (which also owns Killington), manages its snowmaking well and maintains good cover through late spring. The child-care program, integrated with the ski school, operates from a large, attractive center on the slopes. Candor requires us to mention the weekend crush at Mount Snow. If a mountain has both good skiing and ready access to New York, should one expect solitude?

Resort Life

Vermont's Route 100 runs north from Wilmington to West Dover and on to Mount Snow. All along this road and its tributaries are restaurants, clothing and crafts shops. Two handsome country inns, the Inn at Sawmill Farm and the Hermitage have distinguished dining rooms. The village of Wilmington has managed to guard its old wooden New England structures, with the traditional pub such as the Old Red Mill remaining centers for after-ski and evening social life.

The community supports several cross country centers at the Hermitage, the White House and at Timber Creek as well as services such as sleigh rides and snowmobiling.

New condominiums have been built on the mountain and directly opposite the entrance to the base area. Of these, the most complete and luxurious compound is Timber Creek.

Mountain Statistics: Vertical, 1700 feet; Hourly Uphill Lift Capacity, 22,375 skiers; Skiing Terrain, 369 acres, 75 trails.

TIMBER CREEK

WEST DOVER, VT

Timber Creek came as a complete surprise to us, refuting our outmoded ideas of what a mailing address in West Dover, Vermont can be expected to mean. To us, the name "West Dover" had been a visual cryptograph, producing a mental slide show of a handsome New England hamlet, fine old houses, and a tall-spired white colonial church. Then we saw Timber Creek, on

162 acres, with 200 townhouses, racquetball courts, an exercise and weight room, a swimming pool and hot tubs and saunas and cross country trails.

Timber Creek is a major new recreation and condominium endeavor. Its townhouses are large, averaging 2,000 square feet, the rooms are big and numerous, the scale is generous and expansive. Every apartment has a hot tub or sauna, or both, with greenhouse windows facing Mt. Snow. In the kitchen is every popular appliance, including microwave ovens and coffee makers, and all the requisite support tools. Simplicity, Timber Creek knoweth not thy name.

Each townhouse has a direct view of the downhill trails. The Timber Creek shuttle will drop you at Mount Snow and collect you after skiing. Or you may start your cross country tour from your own door, picking up the groomed trail as you pass Timber Creek's ski touring center.

Mount Snow gets a boost by the arrival in the neighborhood of such a dynamic and stylish new vacation community.

OKEMO MOUNTAIN

LUDLOW, VERMONT

In the early 1980s, Okemo consisted in large measure of poma lifts on the slopes and a child-care center at the base. Now Okemo Mountain is dominated by triple and quadruple chair lifts and the base area has a modern day-lodge, condominiums, restaurants and a reception center. Okemo is bigger, more complex and more sophisticated, but still attentive to the skiing family, particularly those with small children.

The Skiing

Okemo has become an excellent mountain for cruisers. With 2,150 feet of vertical, broad trails that sweep top to bottom, and 360 acres of terrain, experts and intermediates can soar around the mountain. In 1987-88, Okemo added the Solitude Peak area with a 5,000 foot quad chair. The new terrain supplemented extensive intermediate slopes, but did not add bumps or steeps; mogul skiing is confined to the upper eastern corner on the Summit chair. Novices can start on the broad bottom slopes, but soon take on the gradual four and a half mile run from the summit.

Consistent with its appeal to families, Okemo provides free skiing for children up to six years old, free child-care during the week and free beginner lift service, regardless of age. Great emphasis is placed on ski school, particularly for children.

Okemo has entered snowmaking's big leagues, covering more than 80 percent of its trails with man-made snow. This supplements a good natural average snow fall of close to 200 inches.

Resort Life

The mountain overlooks the town of Ludlow, a mile from the base lodge. The ski area built 600 condominium apartments, a bar, restaurant and child-care center right at the base of the slopes, thereby creating a unified mountain community. Skiers turn to Ludlow for the best restaurant in the area, the Governor's Inn, and the best entertainment spot, the Pot Belly, both of which are located on Main Street. Eight miles north on Route 100 in the town of Plymouth is Hawk's River Tavern restaurant, worth the journey.

Mountain Statistics: Vertical, 2,150 feet; Hourly Uphill Lift Capacity, 13,400 skiers; Skiing Terrain, 360 Acres, 68 Trails.

WINTERPLACE

LUDLOW, VT

In its recent growth, Okemo built three clusters of condominiums on the mountain. At the base is The Okemo Mountain Lodge, efficient one bedroom apartments with immediate access to the restaurant and child-care center. A few hundred feet above the base is Kettle Brook, comfortable two bedroom apartments. The third cluster has the largest and best appointed apartments, Winterplace.

Winterplace is located at the top of the Mountain Quad, a base service lift which gives access to chairs that run to the top. The condominiums looks onto Okemo and out over the Black River Valley below.

Close to, but separate from the action at the base, Winterplace has the sense of the solitude of the mountain once the lifts close. Residents here enjoy the advantage of Okemo's only indoor swimming pool and hot tub. The spa building, in the middle of the 250 apartments, is the social center and after-ski meeting place for both children and adults.

The architecture of Winterplace is rustic post-modern, suited to its wooded site. The apartments are spacious and bright, with marble fireplaces, cathedral ceilings and sky lights. Light-colored modern furniture promotes the contemporary design and organization of the apartments.

Winterplace apartments, from one to four bed-rooms (some with lofts), fit skiing families, whatever their size. Friendly open kitchens encourage congenial family meals, fireplaces foster relaxed sociability. Without congestion on the slopes and without highway traffic, family members can ski conveniently and on their own schedule. All of Okemo's trails funnel back to one base area, just below Winterplace so children will easily find their way home. Parents needn't worry. Sounds like a vacation to us.

KILLINGTON SKI RESORT

Dodge the numbers or they'll crush you: six mountains, 18 lifts including five quads, 38 miles of trails with snowmaking, 107 trails, 220 days of skiing a season, 250 miles from New York City, 300 or so instructors, 3,000 feet of vertical, one and a half million skier visits a year, 30,163,270 vertical transport feet an **hour**, and gross revenues exceeded only by the federal deficit. But Killington is much more than numbers. It is a great success because it offers skiers of every stripe a variety of terrain found nowhere else in the East, with snow cover of both breadth and quality not surpassed anywhere in the East.

The Skiing

You can't ski numbers, but if you are an expert you can ski Cascade, Superstar, East Fall, Snake Pit, and Outer Limits. These runs are not as long as Stowe's, but for bumps, good fall lines, variety and quick return access, they are the equal of any. For an intermediate, the choice of runs at Killington is a dream. The mountains are so extensive and complicated that you can get lost and stay lost, skiing all the time. Every day can be an adventure – just don't end up at the wrong parking lot at the end of the day.

Novices can start on Snowshed, the basic training slope, which we think has too many lifts. After two days or so, they can head out on their own, taking the Great Eastern trail from Killington Peak all the way, 10.2 miles, to the base of the gondola. Even novices can have adventures.

Resort Life

A mountain village has never developed at Killington. Skiers' essential services (lodging, food, drink, clothes, equipment) are scattered along the access road and on towards Rutland on Route 4. As we write, we expect an extension of the lift system to stretch down to the golf course, which will give ski-in, ski-out access to Highridge (discussed below) and other condominiums.

Health clubs and swimming pools are only available as a right of residence at your hotel or condominium. Indoor tennis is available in Rutland and Woodstock, each about 20 minutes away.

Killington has several good restaurants, Churchills, Hemingway's, and Hawk's River Tavern among them, and a couple of good bars with dancing, The Night Spot and the long-established Wobbly Barn.

At the top of the access road in the Snowshed area are clusters of condominiums, typically solid, comfortable, and utilitarian. Up the hill a bit,and up the scale a lot, is Highridge, on Roaring Brook Road, expected to be ski-in, ski-out shortly. The Woods, another distinguished property, is just off the access road. The elegant Hawk Mountain Inn and Mountain Resort is eight miles south of the Northeast Passage chairlift entrance to Killington.

Mountain Statistics: Vertical, 3,160 feet; Hourly uphill lift capacity, 30,827 skiers; Skiing Terrain, 107 trails, 721 acres.

HIGHRIDGE

KILLINGTON, VT

By itself, Highridge raises the standard of living on the mountain. This is just what Killington needed, cosmopolitan on-slope housing the equivalent of its on-slope ski lift machinery. Killington's earlier array of condominiums were not in themselves unsatisfactory; they simply lacked the pizazz of Highridge. Here is the kind of up-scale, top-dog operation which Killington's Ski Corporation heretofore had not seen fit to develop.

This is the place to be, on the crest of a hill, below the North Brook Gondola Station and above the new golf course. On a large unspoiled tract of land, Highridge is expected to be lift-served, ski-in, ski-out, with the next authorized expansion of the lift system.

The architecture suits both the land on which it lies and the increasingly sophisticated aura of Killington. This is not another series of boxes stacked on boxes, but architect-designed, indeed architect-fussed over. The attention shows in interesting split-level floors, and the use of corners and angles to provide for special uses. Highridge is already winning awards for effective land use, a fact affirmed by the tall trees, boulders and indigenous plantings of its grounds. The magic words for after-ski relaxing, indoor swimming pool and outdoor jacuzzi, are part of Highridge's sports center, which also includes a sauna, game room and tanning room.

All the apartments are lavishly supplied, not only with handsome, stylish furnishings, but also with delightful mechanical goodies, such as microwaves, stereos, and that sturdy servant of the ski vacation, a washer and dryer. The largest apartments, those with four bedrooms and four baths, have VCRs and bumper pool tables, and a map, so you can find your way back to the fireplace in the living room.

THE WOODS AT KILLINGTON

KILLINGTON, VT

This imaginatively planned community, secluded on a hundred acres just off the Killington access road, is composed organically, as though its pieces and parts have emerged from the forest itself. The present complement of houses, townhouses, service buildings and the health club have an affectionate relationship with one another and with the land. As each additional part of the master plan is added, the over-all scheme is increasingly perceptible.

Just outside the gates of The Woods is the helter-skelter building and the hurley-burley business of the ski resort access road, quite different from the orderly, beautiful, tranquil world that lies within. To express the philosophy of The Woods, the sign over the gate should read "Abandon Stress, All You Who Enter Here." This is meant to be a retreat, a shelter from daily strife, knotted stomachs, sweated brows.

Based on a real interest in extending the personal well-being of their guests, The Woods intends ultimately to become an important New England health spa, rehabilitating bruised bodies, abused skin, and jangled nerves alike, in a comprehensive treatment center. Some of the essential components of that therapy, the swimming pool, whirlpool and hot tub, are already available for the pleasure of residents at The Woods. The wooded acres of birch, pine and cedar are themselves a certain therapy.

Like the forest itself, The Woods at Killington grows steadily. From one ski season to the next, the terrain is altered by the newest contributions to the ambitious masterplan. The winter of '89 marked the introduction of Puzant's Restaurant.

Residents at The Woods may choose between an elegant dinner in the restaurant without leaving the grounds or in-room catering without leaving the apartment.

The apartments are luxuriously furnished and fashionably decorated. The kitchens are equipped to the last butter knife and candle holder. The mirrored double jacuzzi in each apartment opened our eyes a bit, but we were reminded of its therapeutic capabilities, when combined with a bottle of wine and two glasses. One may live as elaborately or simply as one likes here.

The Woods at Killington is a major up-scale addition to this spirited, sometimes rambunctious, community. It's also a secret.

HAWK INN AND MOUNTAIN RESORT

PLYMOUTH, VT

The thousand-acre Hawk Inn and Mountain Resort on Route 100, is tactfully situated half way between Okemo, eight miles south, and Killington eight miles north, and you need only choose to which you wish to be conveyed, should you choose to leave.

Are you prepared to leave the health club, one of the best in the ski world? All of the work-out equipment we like to use is assembled here in a Nautilus nirvana: the Nordic Trak, the Lifecycle, the rowing ergometer, and Marci weights. You will have a choice of swimming technologies: you may either swim for distance in the full size heated pool or swim against the current created by jets in the stationary swim lane of the massive hot tub.

Are you sure you want to leave the far-reaching

private cross country trail network that ranges over the mountain and around the lakes of the resort? No crowds, no lift lines, no lift tickets, remember, and Hawk will loan you the equipment.

Leave the horse-drawn sleigh rides? Leave the toboggans and sleds Hawk has here for you? Leave the big skating pond (skates loaned) and the afternoon bonfires?

Should you manage to tear yourself away to go downhill skiing for the day, be back for dinner at The River Tavern, Hawk's elegant restaurant in the Colonial-style building at the base of the mountain (which also includes the health club). Every effort has been made to establish a first class

restaurant here, successfully so. The food is simply terrific and available to you on a breakfast and dinner meal plan.

The condominiums are located at the very top of the resort with views across the valley and adjacent mountains. Each apartment is unique, decorated by its owner with designer unity and an apparently unlimited budget. While there are only 39 condominiums, they range in size from studios to four bedrooms. Most have large stone fireplaces and decks facing over the valley.

Even before you leave home, the Hawk staff anticipate the details important to your satisfaction. Travel directions, program particulars, and a food shopping list for you to order from arrive by mail, followed by a phone call to arrange babysitting, restaurant and ski equipment reservations, and to say a word of welcome. Your apartment lights are turned on before you appear, the fireplace is ready to light with the strike of a match.

You will find yourself waited on hand and foot. The Hawk staff will deliver groceries to your apartment in advance of your arrival, and with proper notice, will arrange for a master chef to come in and prepare a special meal for you. Perhaps you would like a massage? The fire started? Your Christmas tree decorated? A postage stamp? Just ask.

The only thing the staff at Hawk Resort won't help you do, is to leave. That won't be easy.

PICO SKI RESORT

RUTLAND, VT

Now half a century old, Pico is once again a big story. In Vermont in 1937, only Mount Mansfield attracted more attention from skiers. During the next 49 years, Pico grew with deliberate speed, overshadowed by its aggressive neighbor. Pico's Golden Anniversary provided the impetus to step out of Killington's shadow and claim its birthright as a major Vermont ski resort.

Construction of the Golden Express high speed detachable quad in 1987 brought the lift system up to date. At the base of the lifts, a mountain village began to take shape, incorporating the most effective components of modern American and European ski resorts.

Expansion on the mountain continued in 1988 with the installation of yet another detachable quad, practically a declaration of war by historically soft-spoken Pico. This made Pico only the second resort in the East to have two detachable quads. It also increased the number of its lifts to seven chairs and two surface lifts, with an hourly uphill capacity of 13,000 skiers, a promise that for the time being lines will be short at Pico. Pico's snowmaking now covers 82 percent of its terrain, a challenge on another front.

In 1989, Pico will complete construction of a major sports center, the final piece in the elaborated Golden Anniversary plan to rethink and reposition the resort.

Pico now has an attractive, complete mountain village and a state-of-the-art lift system. That's news.

The Skiing

The mountain is long and gentle. The Golden Express rises 1,967 feet from base to summit, giving access to intermediate terrain and to two short expert runs. Near the bottom on the left, a short chair serves a steep mogul run and several other intermediate runs. On the right is the latest detachable quad, serving a well-segregated novice and lower-intermediate area.

Pico is an excellent mountain for beginners and for improving skiers. The slope of the terrain invites you to work on carving your turns; the excellent ski school does, too. Among the staff are several of the East's top training and technical pros. The ski school has a separate racing division, providing concentrated instruction, season-long programs and frequent events for both child and adult racers.

Mountain Statistics: Vertical, 1,967 feet; Hourly Uphill Lift Capacity, 13,000 skiers; Skiing Terrain, 35 trails.

PICO RESORT HOTEL

When the Sports Center opens, Pico's little community will be a complete winter vacation center. All the essentials of life have been provided within walking distance of the apartments. To buy groceries, to play tennis, to swim, to socialize after skiing, or to dine out require only that you put on your coat, not find your car keys.

At the Sports Center is a 75 foot lap pool. The aerobics room is specially designed for effective group exercise, built with a special floor too complicated for our understanding. The weight room has the latest punishing machines. The 1988-89 season will inaugurate indoor racquet sports at Pico, including tennis, racquetball and squash.

Pico's village is so modern that it features the latest ski resort lodging configurations, the so-called "condotel." This beastly portmanteau word is meant to suggest an amalgam between condominium (meaning, in itself, an apartment) and hotel. The Pico Resort Hotel at the base of the mountain is one such. The hotel is a single building with guest rooms to left and right off a central corridor. It has a twenty-four hour front desk. Half the accommodations are hotel rooms, a bath and bedroom.

The remainder are condominiums (meaning apartments), meaning large studios with a full kitchen at one end, a fireplace and sitting area with a fold-out bed at the other, and a dining table between.

The studio apartment permits its occupants to prepare some or all of their meals, make their own jolly, fire-lit after-ski parties, and have a snack in the middle of the night if the whim strikes.

The minor genius of the whole operation is that the hotel rooms can be opened to the studios, creating a large one bedroom apartment with hotel services.

You may vow to economize and cook dinner every night, but the pizza shop you pass at street level will deliver to your door, if you find yourself too weak to walk, let alone heat soup, after skiing all day.

Seasons, the base lodge restaurant, across the plaza towards the lifts, will threaten your resolve further with a big made-to-order breakfast or an up-scale white tablecloth dinner when your hard day's playing is done.

Pico is compact and uncrowded, built to a scale comfortable for children. In fact, Pico has about it an echo of summer camp in a winterized, grown-up edition. The mountain, the dining halls, the sports centers are here to keep you busy and happy until you crawl between the sheets. The difference? No revelry and no counselors with whistles.

SUGARBUSH SKI RESORT

WARREN, VT

Sugarbush is one of the most balanced resorts in New England. It has good terrain for all skiers, one of the best and most inclusive on-mountain developments, and a complete range of accommodations.

The Skiing

Sugarbush resort has two mountains, South Basin (formerly known as Sugarbush Mountain), and Mount Ellen, (formerly the Glenn Ellen ski resort). True to its name, South Basin is laid out around a bowl. At the bottom on the left is short, steep, true fall line expert terrain, with two very challenging runs, Stein's and The Mall. Running up the center of the basin, in an area once served by a 9,000 foot gondola, are two chairs accessing expert and intermediate runs.

To the right of these chairs is Castle Rock, with four old-fashioned New England trails: narrow, twisting, tricky. One of these runs, Rumble, with its sharp corners, quick drops, glades and an occasional rock, tree or fallen skier, can be one of the most amusing challenges in New England skiing. On the right of the basin, served by a chair and poma lift in tandem, is more intermediate terrain and, to the extreme right of the basin, next to the Village is a small novice area, well segregated from the other terrain.

The second ski center, Mount Ellen, has a huge vertical of 2600 feet, with terrain that changes dramatically from steep to flat. Experts and intermediates will enjoy the short but steep upper lift. Novices can wander around the outer trails served by the long, long bottom lift.

Resort Life:

Our enthusiasm for Sugarbush is further stimulated by the excellent facilities in the Village at the base of South Basin. Although small, with only a few shops and restaurants, a child-care center and a major indoor sports center, the Village provides the community core for the surrounding condominiums. Two restaurants in the Village, Chez Henri and Phoenix, are excellent. You can manage nicely here without a car.

Mountain Statistics: Vertical (Mt. Ellen), 2,600 feet; (South Basin), 2,300 feet; Hourly Uphill Lift Capacity, 16,500 skiers; Skiing Terrain, 68 trails.

MOUNTAINSIDE

WARREN, VT

Mountainside is positioned nicely, just above Sugarbush Village and just above a ski trail. Children can be left for the day at the Valley Day School, (pictured above) a snowball's throw from Mountainside, where they'll get acquainted with skis their size and the business of getting around on them. Valley Day School is modestly proud that several of their former peanuts have gone on to ski for the USA in the Olympics, although they don't make promises or offer guarantees. The kids are happy to be there, which may be the secret to making champions.

Ski home on Out To Lunch at noon for tomato soup and peanut butter and jam sandwiches, one of the great sports lunches and reason enough to take up skiing. A few adjustments and you're off again.

The kitchen is a part of the larger living area in these practical, attractive apartments. Each has a front balcony, permitting parent-to-child communication without requiring ski removal. The balcony also permits air delivery of dry mittens, spare change and those peanut butter sandwiches to children standing below.

The location permits quick forays to the small grocery store and encourages attendance at the adjacent restaurant, Chez Henri. This small bistro gets going after skiing, accelerates through the dinner hour, and goes late, becoming a disco, occasionally with a small band.

We think it possible and not inconvenient to stay here without a car, using the shuttle bus to get around the valley, if we need to leave the Village or the South Basin. Truth is, we don't bother to leave.

PARADISE

WARREN, VT

Overheard in the Sugarbush Sports Center: "Do you know where Paradise is?" "Is this some kind of religion question?" "Not exactly. I'm looking for my friends' condominium, called Paradise. They said it's in Sugarbush Village, near The Phoenix restaurant."

"At least we know then why it's called Paradise."

We later learned from better informed hot tub companions that Paradise actually is in Sugarbush Village, located just a little past the Sport Center, on Inferno Road. Allusions to eternity aside, Paradise is a cluster of agreeable two-bedroom apartments, well-appointed and well-decorated by their owners.

Outside the Bauhaus style prevails, boxy with wood trim. Inside, the rooms are large, with a cathedral ceiling and a raised- hearth fireplace in the living room. The second floor balcony overlook-

ing the living area is repeated outside in a balcony overlooking the forest behind the property.

In the center of the cluster is the Paradise penthouse, an after-ski social center for those residents who have had enough exercise for the day. Others should report to the Sugarbush Sports Center, a two-minute walk, the site for water-based after-ski relaxation or vigorous exercise training. The Sports Center is one of the best in the ski world, with three indoor tennis courts, two squash courts, two racquetball courts, an indoor pool, hot tub, steam room, an elaborate exercise room, and an extensive training and aerobic program. It also has a lounge for an after-exercise drink.

After a work-out and a swim, you'll be ready to test the hypothesis that The Phoenix is next to Paradise. The restaurant is rightly famous in the ski world for its "chocolate, chocolate, chocolate." You'll have to walk over, but you won't have to walk back. The shrimp are good and the duck is wonderful, but it is the desserts that transport patrons at the Phoenix to, well, Paradise.

SNOW CREEK

WARREN, VT

The apartments in Snow Creek are like a smooth stone tossed about until all the rough edges are worn off. This is not a design experiment nor innovative iffy technology. Instead we have in Snow Creek the profit-taking of the vacation lodging trials and tests. This works, simply, sanely, sensibly.

Two bedrooms, two baths in each apartment. Maybe other combinations are available elsewhere, but this works the best. At Snow Creek, you won't find a large Mommy and Daddy Bear bedroom and a little one for Baby Bear, but two about equal size, neither enormous. You're expected to sleep here, not entertain. And because they are equal, two couples can compatibly share the apartment without begging each other's forgiveness for bedroom inequity. Even children will be pleased to receive equal treatment.

The kitchen is open to the dining and living area. The people who prepare the meals shouldn't be relegated in disgrace to the kitchen cell. They should be center stage. They should be able to hold court while tending the pots and pans. The open kitchen works at Snow Creek.

A washer and dryer, no quarters, no waiting. Life and a ski vacation are both too short to be running up and down stairs to see if the long underwear is dry yet. Having the mechanical devices within the apartment works.

Of course, there is a fireplace, the kind to get warm by, to gather around, to stare into, the kind where a careful child could toast a marshmallow after dinner. The warm glow of fire works.

The Snow Creek condominiums are where skiers would like them to be, which is to say a few yards from the lift. The price of this exalted location is that Snow Creek residents have a seven-minute walk to Sugarbush Village and its associated services and restaurants. However, they are immediately adjacent to the Spring Fling lift, the highest base lift at South Basin. This lift provides quick access to the Valley Chair and some of the best skiing on the mountain. Ski-in, ski-out. Why not? It works.

SOUTHFACE

WARREN, VT

From the penthouse bedroom on the third floor, above the tops of the birches and maple trees that surround the building, you can look over the golf course to the hills forty miles away at the far end of Mad River Valley. West a mile, you can see the trails on South Basin: Spring Fling, Stein's Run and the Mall. But here at Southface, with the sun streaming in the window, it's so quiet you could almost hear yourself think.

Southface articulates modern Yankee ethics.

Early New England settlers had no shame espousing a doctrine of economy: "Use it up, wear it out, make do." At first glance, the frank luxury of Southface may not seem friendly to thriftiness, but closer scrutiny uncovers the architectural elements of passive solar power.

The townhouses are three stories high, with floor-to-ceiling glass on the southern exterior to allow the greatest exposure to the sun. Heat is gathered from black slate floor panels next to the

windows and stored until needed in water cylinders hidden in the walls. While you're off skiing, heat is collected so you'll be warm when you get home. Mr. Thoreau would think it a little fancy, but we like it.

The middle floor includes the entry from the carport and the Great Room, where people preparing the meal in the kitchen area are not socially cut off from those sitting around the fire in the living area. The couch potatoes will have no trouble hearing a gentle request to get up, please, and set the table.

We like the way the space works for the group and we like the way it works for sub-groups. We appreciate the recessed two-person hot tub on the ground floor, separate from the Great Room a floor above, with a private view of the forest outside.

Perhaps Mr. Thoreau was never invited into a bubbling hot tub at the end of a hard day of skiing to discuss the condition of the universe. It might have changed his whole way of thinking.

MAD RIVER GLEN

WAITSFIELD, VT

O n the peak just north of Mount Ellen is the legendary Mad River Glen, realizing its Yankee mythology year after year.

The Skiing
The Single Chair, installed in 1947, is still *the* lift to the summit, providing access to Chute and Paradise, the former a profusion of bumps, the latter a profusion of trees, both steep and treacherous. Any route from the top of the single chair entails an initial sharp drop, demanding concentration and fancy foot work.

A double chair (circa 1962. May we say "new"?) to a lesser peak and the warming-hut serves intermediate trails embellished with the occasional snare or ambush. Novices, unavoidably slighted here, may seek out accommodating terrain off the lower Birdland chair. Mad River Glen is inappropriate for beginners, to say the least.

The latest trends in intensive mountain management are determinedly ignored at Mad River. Quads with padded chairs and matching foot rests are unthinkable. Snowmaking is disparaged. "Skiers want to ski natural snow, not instant hardpack," says Betsy Pratt, Yankee owner of this venerable institution. Despite her commitment to nature, recently a few snow guns around the base abet fickle nature.

But neither Pisten Bullies nor snowmaking will pave your course from the top. It is just you, your skis, and natural snow in the condition left by skiers before you. Truth in skiing.

Resort Life
Mad River Glen shares the rich common resources of the Mad River Valley with its newer (1962) neighbors. Skiers staying in the immediate vicinity of the mountain (Waitsfield at Route 17) have a different perspective from that of Sugarbush skiers, who are closer to Sugarbush Village and Warren. Two inns in Waitsfield have outstanding restaurants, Tucker Hill Lodge and the Waitsfield Inn. Tucker Hill is also a major cross country center. The town of Waitsfield is skier-focused, with plenty of services, good antique shops, and Gallager's, one of the oldest dancing spots in New England skiing.

Mountain Statistics: Vertical, 2,000 feet; Hourly uphill lift capacity, 3,000 skiers; Skiing Terrain, 30 trails.

THE BATTLEGROUND

L eave behind the turbulence of busy lives and the irritation of travel as you drive through the long wooden covered bridge over the Mill Brook at the entrance to The Battleground. "Yes kids, we are here." The wooded 60-acre site, enhanced by three brimming streams, dislodges the residue of city images, exchanging soft snow for hard concrete, and tall pines and maple trees for anonymous tall buildings.

The townhouse-style apartments, with sharp

sloping roofs, prominent chimneys, and rough-cut siding are well-suited to the wooded property. Inside, cathedral ceilings confer a sense of openness to the communal areas. The floor-to-ceiling fieldstone fireplace at the heart of each apartment is the skiers' gathering place at the end of the day, the impassive witness to either boasting or self-pity, the sponsor of good cheer and reflective silences alike. In the segregated kitchens are the essential modern appliances, including microwave ovens in some, and all are equipped for preparation of a holiday meal. The traditional dining area lends a proper dignity to Battleground's large apartments.

The townhouses have easy access to the out-of-doors, a substantial part of the pleasure of being here. Cross country trails begin at your door, follow old logging trails, circle the grounds and poke up into the foothills of Mad River Glen.

Two of the cross country trails interconnect with Mad River, so with good snow and a decent map, you can actually ski home. Battleground has an outdoor paddle tennis court, a very New England

THE BATTLEGROUND

answer to elaborate bubbled indoor tennis courts.

These condominiums, with their implicit Mad River connection, their wooded setting, their contemporary, but not glitzy construction, appeal to the educated, ascetic New England or New York family who form the backbone of Mad River's ski clientele. These skiers share with Mad River a suspicion of grooming and snowmaking, of VCR's and microwaves, of hot tubs and saunas. They equate living and growing with forebearing and enduring, and enjoy themselves by working and playing hard. They are more likely to be cross country skiers than couch potatoes. At Battleground, they are at home. Their kids, brought up on tough trails and real snow, skiing on older sibling's cast-off skis, wearing determinedly un-chic ski clothes, promise to maintain these quaint latter-day Puritan values.

Battleground and Mad River, two miles away, go hand in hand. The covered bridge is somewhat like Mad River's single chair: each evidences the solid foundation built for us by earlier generations.

STOWE

Stowe, with its high-steepled church, is the quintessential New England village. Mount Mansfield is one of the most challenging mountains in the United States. Between the town and the mountain along the access road, are the essential ingredients of a ski vacation. This is a first class resort.

The Skiing

When you look up at Mansfield from the parking lot, you know you have arrived at the Mecca of expert Eastern skiing. Just to see the National or the Starr plummeting down, you have to crane your neck up. Then hold your breath. This is great expert terrain, made more so by bumps, hard-packed snow, and icy spots. O.K., so they broadened the National and cut off its top. They broadened Panic Alley, too. Maybe it's not as it used to be in the old days – they make snow now – but it is closer to vintage Stowe than management would have it.

Intermediates will find both opportunity and challenge at Stowe, on the chairs (one a high-speed quad) and on the nearby gondola. The runs all drop 2,000 feet, so even if these skiers avoid such intermediate traps as the wall on Hayride, their legs will register the journey.

Novices have a choice of the lower portions of Spruce Peak, across the road from Mt. Mansfield, or the long winding Toll Road from the top of Mansfield. This ski area is only moderately accommodating to novices. However, on the lower left side (when looking up) is an improved area for family skiing. The new chair from the Inn at the Mountain (formerly the Toll House area) tying the Toll House slope into the Mansfield runs permits skiers of dramatically different abilities, novice to expert, to meet for lunch without leaving the mountain. Mansfield is becoming slightly more skier-friendly.

Of late, the Mansfield Company has been outpaced by its southern competitors, but we hear of improvements to come. Snowmaking has already improved. There are even elaborate discussions of a base lodge at the bottom of Mansfield with elevator service to the chair lifts, ending the present crawl and stumble approach. We know New England: changes will not occur overnight, as management must balance the values and traditions of the past against the needs of the future.

Resort Life

Stowe has a deserved reputation for first rate restaurants, among them Ten Acres, Green Mountain Inn, Isle de France in Stowe and Villa Tragara in Waterbury Center. After skiing, the Matterhorn is a must, and at night, The Rusty Nail is the place for the young and B.K. Clarks the spot for the formerly so. For an after-dinner drink, perhaps with music, we like Charlie B's at the Stoweflake or the bar at Topnotch.

On the less formal side, the Pub and the Shed have atmospheres that are conducive to long lunches. Trattoria La Festa is a good, inexpensive Italian restaurant which makes its own pasta. The town of Stowe, while small, has interesting shops selling items of all sorts from antiques to videos. If you get bored with these in-town diversions, a tour of Ben and Jerry's ice cream factory, 10 miles south will keep you and the kids amused.

Stowe has everything for the non-skiing athlete. Four cross country centers with interconnected trails put Stowe in the exclusive league with Jackson, N.H.. There is indoor tennis at Topnotch, an extensive health club in town open to the public, and movies and special shows at night. With any luck, Alan Schonberger, the adorable ski mime, will be performing.

When you're tired of Stowe, you're tired of skiing.

Mountain Statistics: Vertical, 2,350 feet; Hourly Uphill Lift Capacity, 9,233 skiers; Skiing Terrain, 43 trails, 385 acres.

THE LODGE AT STOWE

STOWE, VT

The Lodge at Stowe, at the top of the access road and the foot of the Toll House slope on Mount Mansfield, is one of three components of an informal compound. The Lodge provides traditional, home-like vacation apartments. The Inn at the Mountain offers a good restaurant and modern hotel rooms. The Health Club contri-

butes the after-ski meeting site for both, with a group hot tub, an exercise room, and conference space. These three related institutions form a triangle around a common open space, punctuated by willows and pines.

The scale and tenor of the Lodge apartments are grown-up, tasteful, upper-middle class, even

refined. There is a nice understated air of gentility, not grand, heaven forbid, but modestly self-assured. These apartments were built to last, as solid as the granite face of Stowe. No wide open Great Rooms here. This is not Trendsville, this is old New England. You'll get a living room, dining room, and kitchen, and the kitchen will be sufficiently equipped and large enough to prepare a meal considerable more elaborate than coffee and toast.

The Lodge apartments, now a decade old, are emerging, one by one, from their first full round of major redecorating. Apartment owners do the decorating themselves, for themselves, with varying effects and success, but invariably in good taste.

Just the other side of the Health Club is the Toll House Lift, named for the Health Club's earlier incarnation. The Lodge and The Inn at the Mountain are the primary ski-in, ski-out accommodattions on Mount Mansfield. The Inn, the Lodge, and the Health Club combined give Stowe an attractive, interactive little on-mountain community.

STONYBROOK RESORT

STOWE, VT

Stonybrook has about it a rustic beauty, fostered by the old stone walls and the pastoral grace of the Spears' farm. The townhouses are tucked into the edge of the forest, set back and camouflaged from the road by thick maples and tall fir trees. In a precedent-making conservation effort, two-fifths of the total Stonybrook property, some 60 acres, has been deeded to perpetual agricultural use. The Spears, who sold the parcel, have life use of their farmhouse. The land, now farmed by their son under a long lease, confers seasonal serenity on the view from

the townhouses across the farm to Mount Mansfield.

This townhouse community consists of 50 townhouses (80 eventually) a community center, and a swimming pool. At the community center, children can meet each other in the recreation room and join the adults in the large group jacuzzi. Just across Luce Road, the Stowe cross country trail,

leading from the village to the Topnotch Ski Touring Center, parallels the Stonybrook property. Cross country skiers may use the village trail without charge, either as a route to Topnotch and its cross country trail network, or as a discrete route itself.

The townhouses are frankly large, averaging over 2,000 square feet. In each living room is a massive fieldstone fireplace and cathedral ceiling. The kitchen contains every culinary appurtenance, tendering an invitation and a challenge to any chef usually hampered by a city-sized worksite. The largest edition of these three-story townhouses contains five or six bedrooms, dispersed astutely on each floor. In some versions, the master bedroom boasts a fireplace, which is to us the next to last word in gentle living.

By and large, the owners of the individual townhouse have made tasteful interior decoration choices, each a creative contribution to Stonybrook's sense of rural luxury. Many of the apartments have a large private glassed-in jacuzzi at ground level with a matchless view of the adjoining fields and neighboring Mount Mansfield. In the language of rural luxury, this is the last word.

STOWEFLAKE RESORT

STOWE, VT

Stoweflake's apartments were conceived along lines very close to our own way of thinking, so naturally we think they are brilliant. The design is a modified, modernized Colonial saltbox in gray clapboard with white trim, a look reminiscent of Cape Cod. Adaption of the saltbox design to suit the site and circumstance created a private patio and entryway carved out of the long roof line at ground level, as well as a balcony cut from the second story.

Yankee references continue inside. Before the relatively recent days of central oil heat, fuel came from trees felled, cut in lengths, and split by axe, no mean task. Heat was an expensive, precious resource, not to be squandered on rooms with no occupants.

We traced that thinking in the Stoweflake apartments, which consist of two separate, unequal parts. The larger portion is a full apartment in its own right, with a full kitchen open to the dining area and a comfortable living room with a brick raised-hearth fireplace. Upstairs are several bedrooms off a hallway open to the living room below.

To the left of the ground floor entry is the second smaller part of the whole, a large bedroom fitted out as snugly as a yacht, containing a miniature, serviceable kitchen, a small table and a sitting area. The two may be combined as a whole or divided into two separate apartments, depending upon the taste and size of the group. Yankee forebearers would approve the thrift afforded by a correct match.

Stoweflake is located right off the Mountain Road about half way between the village of Stowe and Mt. Mansfield. This area is the heart of Stowe's after-ski life. Passing by the property is Stowe's mountain-to-village cross country trail. You can take off from here and ski to any of Stowe's four cross country centers or beyond, north to Smugglers Notch or south to Bolton Valley. For the trip to Smugglers we suggest you take the chair up Spruce Peak. For the trip to Bolton, through the Trapp Family Lodge network of trails, we suggest a guide. Before you take on either of these adventures, let us urge that you get in great shape.

A car is useful at Stoweflake and in Stowe generally, although it is not necessary. Free trolley service runs up and down the Mountain Road throughout the day at 30-minute intervals between the village and the mountain. The health center is across a field from the apartments, worth a trip for the indoor swimming pool, exercise room, group jacuzzi and sauna. In the adjacent rec room is a pool table and a television lounge for the deeply addicted. Stoweflake may lure you away from your own kitchen with meal plans at Winfield's in the main building or a Stowe Dine-around deal. Either way, after skiing or after dinner, put Stoweflake's low key skiers' hangout, Charlie B's, into your evening's plans. Old photos of Stowe legends on the walls remind you this isn't just any ski resort.

BOLTON VALLEY SKI RESORT

BOLTON, VT

Bolton Valley is a hidden treasure, a tiny mountain community just 20 minutes from the Burlington airport, snuggled into a basin at 2,150 feet, about 1,000 feet higher than New England's other ski mountains. Within the basin is a complete, if small, resort, with two hotels, five condominium clusters, a trail-side inn, restaurants, and a full-scale sports center with a swimming pool, racquetball courts, exercise rooms and two indoor tennis courts.

The Skiing

In 1988, Bolton expanded its vertical to 1,540 feet by adding a high-speed quad, which starts well below the base lodge area. This quad serves trails cut to modern tastes – broad, rolling, man-made snow-covered, Western-style trails. The new terrain adds balance to the "old" mountain, on which are preserved a couple of classic twisters that can make intermediates squirm and experts nervous. Bump areas are short and sweet. The juxtaposition of the old and new provides skiers of all abilities a sufficient menu to keep them on their toes.

Bolton is more dependant than other mountains on natural snow but its elevation is considerably higher. It averages close to 275 inches per year, second in New England, we think, to Jay Peak. As Bolton is still something of an insider secret, slopes and trails are lightly skied, preserving the snow and preventing lift lines.

Supplementing Bolton's five chair lifts is the Mighty Mite, an old-fashioned rope tow with handles, open and free to first time skiers. Kids won't get lost or run over in this playland. First rate ski instructors for children stay with their charges all day. Bolton's night skiing introduces a different perspective to the mountain and gives children the chance to demonstrate, under the stars, their new proficiency.

Resort Life

In the central U-shaped building are two hotels, the Lodge and Chateau, each with a restaurant and shops. The condominium clusters are distributed around the base area, none very far from the main buildings. Restaurants offer a variety of nourishment, from pizza up to the excellent Lindsay's Restaurant. After dinner, the James Moore Tavern, at the end of one leg of the U, becomes a low-key music club.

Bolton makes evenings easy for parents. In addition to its day nursery program, it has an evening nursery for kids under 6, and a Pied Piper activities program three nights a week for those 6 to 11.

The Sports Center, just down the hill from the central building, has a friendly bar adjacent to the pool, presenting a tough after-ski decision. Bolton also has a 100 K network of cross country trails which wander around, below and above the village. An adventurous skier can go right over the top, and with effort and guidance, find his way into the Trapp Family Lodge cross country network at Stowe.

We took a few runs on our teleskis at Bolton. The resort welcomes all forms of quiet free expression.

Trailside condominiums

Bolton is owned and run by the DesLauriers family. The DesLauriers dynasty now governs 6,000 acres, the Bolton Valley ski village and 140 condominiums. They didn't have to ask an outside consultant what a family on a ski vacation would like.

The apartment should be uncomplicated. Hence, furniture and interior design were chosen to provide easy comfort and to abide normal use. Mini-laundromats are in each building.

Convenience is important. The Sports Club condominiums are right next to the Sports Center. The Wentworth are right next to lift 3. Courtside are next to the cross country trail, and Lift-line are at lift 1. And they are all close to the hotel, the grocery store, the restaurants, cafeteria and the ski school.

A vacation should be a vacation for everyone in the family, so Bolton offers meal plans to supplement the well-equipped kitchens. A vacation should bring the family together in the evening, thus every apartment has a fireplace in the living room and a stack of wood outside. Bring your own set of checkers.

Mountain statistics: Vertical, 1540 feet; Hourly Uphill Lift Cap., 6000 skiers; Skiing Terrain, 80 acres.

SMUGGLERS' NOTCH

SMUGGLERS' NOTCH, VT

In the mountains above Smugglers' Notch remain scattered secret caves, the warehouses and hideouts of contraband smugglers during the War of 1812. The trails now used by skiers on Sterling, Madonna, and Morse mountains correspond to the paths of clandestine tradesmen moving goods over the mountains to Canada. Now families hide away here for a week at a time, to ski, to ride, to play, to relax.

The Skiing

The steep rocky contours of Madonna Mountain dictate narrow, wandering trails, criss-crossing the fall line, genuine expert terrain over a vertical of 2,100 feet.

Sterling (which backs on and is interconnected into Stowe's Spruce Peak), is a well-cut intermediate mountain with one long novice trail, Rum Runner. Morse, the small novice area, is immediately above the village, its gentle pitch well-suited for learning.

Resort Life

After a quarter century of rehearsal, the assortment of restaurants, sports facilities, apartments, and programs at the Village of Smugglers' Notch match almost perfectly the needs and wishes of skiing families. Smugglers' pioneers are now introducing their own children to the discreet charms of the sport of skiing as practiced here.

The village is compact and largely car-free, so children can wander by themselves, the ultimate luxury these days. The new, million-dollar childcare center, Alice's Wonderland, introduces little ones to each other and to skiing. Families choose between their own cooking and that of the three convenient, suitable restaurants. The village also has a general store, selling basic groceries and skiing *et ceteras*.

Smugglers' knows some people don't ski, and some don't ski every day. Non-skiers are beguiled with three exceptional alternatives: tennis on the

bubble-covered courts, cross country skiing on the extensive groomed trails, and riding on spirited saddle horses. Of course, they can also swim, take a jacuzzi, or workout in the small gym.

All of these facilities and the mountain itself are under one management, included in soup-to-nuts packages providing bed, board, sports, lessons and lifts in a variety of combinations. Villmark-sauna, an apartment cluster, is at the edge of the woods with a view over the top of the village. The living room is large, with a nice fireplace and comfortable furniture. The two bedrooms and baths, equal size, are at opposite ends of the apartment, a good layout for couples sharing.

Families vacationing at Smugglers' can go skat-ing, join in building a bonfire, cross country ski by moonlight, dress-up and go out for dinner, send world-weary teenagers out to meet each other at Entertainment Alley, make popcorn and watch a movie, get up early for first tracks, sleep 'till noon, just relax and enjoy each other. Some even go skiing.

Mountain Statistics: Vertical, 2,610; Hourly uphill lift capacity, 4,175; Skiing Terrain, 41 trails, 55 miles.

JAY PEAK SKI RESORT

JAY, VT

Jay Peak is one of the high points – literally – in Vermont's Northeast Kingdom, a cluster of three counties characterized by open valleys and rolling hills. The roads to Jay Peak from the west, Routes 105 and 242 which cross the top of the state, are recognized for their tranquility and pastoral charm.

Jay Peak provides good skiing, good snow, short lift lines and convenient housing. The mountain is big, but the resort is compact, spare, practical. It's still "country" here.

The Skiing

Jay has Vermont's only tram, as warm a route to the top as we know. The tram is the avenue to tricky intermediate trails with odd fall lines, great views, and unexpected intersections.

In 1988, Jay opened a new quad chair to a peak just below the top of the tram. Under it, Jay cut a 150-foot wide "super trail," straightened out several of the old runs, and gave that tract modern, true fall-line skiing.

Completely segregated from this tram/quad area is an expert mountain served by a triple chair. With four steep, straight runs, a vertical of 1,200 feet, this is one of the best expert areas in the East. Two or three of these runs are allowed to bump up. Resilient skiers can pound away, up and down, up and down, bashing knees, backs and brains with no time wasted on run-outs or run-arounds.

Jay's skiing is balanced and interesting. Snow-making supplements its 300 inches of natural snow – the most in the East – and it's a best bet for short lift lines.

Resort Life

The Tyrolean chalet at the base of the tram is the day-lodge, equipped with bar and restaurant. The Hotel Jay next door (good restaurant) and the condominiums along the trails provide on-mountain lodging.

Slopeside

For families with young children, we just don't know a better place than Jay Peak. Having struggled ourselves with the costs of out-fitting, ticketing and teaching our kids to ski, we haven't figured out yet how we managed back then and we haven't a clue how young families do it today.

We are not alone. When Bill Stenger, father of three, became Jay Peak's General Manager a few years ago, he saw the ski world in a refreshingly new way, wearing parent glasses over a businessman's eyes. He determined that Jay Peak would reinforce young families' skiing inclinations with policies that encouraged them to ski more easily and more often.

While staying on the mountain, either at Hotel Jay or in the condominiums, children two and up are guests at Kinderschool from nine o'clock to four in the afternoon in the Austrian Haus. That's rather nice, but that's not all. After four, child-care operations shift to the Hotel Jay, with supervised dinner at the Children's Table and accompanied play after dinner in the game room and family lounge. Children under twelve stay free in the condominiums and the Hotel; kiddies under six also ski free.

Slopeside apartments are just slightly up the mountain from the hotel, beside the Interstate trail. Open the door and they're gone.

Slopeside's kitchens are equipped to prepare even a holiday meal. However, should you grow faint from the effort (or the thought), just down the hill a bit sits the Hotel Jay offering breakfast and

dinner on a reasonably priced meal plan, with the International Restaurant next door in the base lodge as an alternative.

The apartments are modest, practical, and efficient: sturdy furniture, living room with fireplace, washer-dryer, and a balcony looking out over the trail, for supervising, applauding and occasionally sunbathing. We're telling you, Jay Peak knows families.

Mountain Statistics: Vertical, 2,153; Hourly Uphill Lift Cap., 8,400; Skiing Terrain, 35 trails.

LOON MOUNTAIN and SKI 93

LINCOLN, NH

Once ignored by hearty skiers on their way to neighboring Cannon Mountain, Loon has been adopted by Boston's affluent suburban families, who prefer the well-tended trails of Loon to the icy runs at Cannon. Over the past decade, unabated enthusiasm has produced the current boomtown of Lincoln at the base of Loon out of a sleepy country hamlet. Loon is also the center of a range of mountains that includes four other resorts which, together with Loon, form the Ski 93 Association, with interchangeable lift tickets.

The Skiing

Loon abuts the town of Lincoln. The four other mountains, Cannon (north by 20 minutes), Bretton Woods (north by 40 minutes), and Tenney Mountain and Waterville Valley, (each 20 minutes south), are within a short drive.

Loon expects, hopes and prays to be allowed to open adjacent South Mountain in 1989, which will just about double its total terrain. The plans, the interconnecting trails, and pedestrian bridges to the new mountain are all in place.

The expansion is sorely needed. Loon, at present, is a small mountain, with good vertical, 2100 feet. Loon's snowmaking system is strong, its trails are carefully groomed. Expert terrain is limited and not terribly steep. Its special appeal is to teenagers who engage in social skiing on its ubiquitous intermediate runs.

For variety, and a dramatic difference, ski **Cannon Mountain**, the state-run old-style New England skiing gem. With its twisting, often icy runs, its steep Northeast face, and its gentle terrain on the Peabody slopes, Cannon is still a skier's mountain. Not until 1980 did Cannon replace its 1938 tram. True to its own history, Cannon would appear to believe its own myths.

Tenney and **Bretton Woods** are both small, essentially intermediate and novice mountains. Tenney is less than 2 hours from Boston, a savvy alternative, a warm-up depot, or a respite on the way north or south. Bretton is distinguished for its isolation, its magnificent view of Mount Washington, and of glorious old Mount Washington Hotel, (closed, unfortunately, in winter).

Waterville is in itself a complete resort with a 2000 foot vertical and terrain for all skiers. It lacks the expert challenge of Cannon, but its snowmaking assures better cover.

Resort Life (at Loon)

Most of Lincoln is newly built, including its large indoor mall, with a sports center expected adjacent to it. Three miles north is the traditional New England town of North Woodstock with a handsome old inn, several restaurants and a bar or two.

Mountain Statistics: Vertical (for Loon), 2,100 feet; Hourly Uphill Lift Capacity, 9,000 skiers; Skiing Terrain, 22 miles of trails, 234 acres.

RIVERGREEN

All had been quiet along the Pemigewasset River for the past half century, until the development of skiing at Loon brought winter tourists to the White Mountains and to the town of Lincoln.

In front of Rivergreen and the Millfront Marketplace runs the Kancamagus Highway, one of the most spectacular drives in New England. Beside Rivergreen flows the Hancock branch of the Pemigewasset River, a clear mountain stream with scattered sections of rapids.

Rivergreen, a large, handsome post-modern condotel and The Mill House Inn share the responsibility for lodging at The Millfront Marketplace,

RIVERGREEN

with the Inn providing guest rooms and Rivergreen offering both hotel rooms and vacation apartments.

Both the Inn and Rivergreen are part of the larger Millfront Marketplace complex which includes restaurants, stores, movie theaters, a nine-hole golf course/cross country skiing center, the future sports facility, a projected hotel and conference center, and an arts center. Millfront has become the center of Lincoln.

Rivergreen and the Inn also share some important guest amenities, such as the indoor swimming pool and group hot tub at the Inn and the outdoor skating rink next to Rivergreen.

The White Mountains were sighted from the coast by Giovanni da Verrazano in 1524. Settlers arrived in the mid-seventeenth century and were befriended by some Indians, such as Kangamagus, and rightfully cursed by others, such as Chocorua, for whom a nearby mountain is named. New Hampshire in the mid-nineteenth century claimed three natural resources that could profitably be exploited: waterways to provide power, forests to provide lumber or pulp, and Yankee ingenuity to build the factories to use them. Adjacent to Rivergreen is the site of the former J.E. Henry Paper Mill, the remains of which will be incorporated into Rivergreen's new athletic club.

A new bridge over the Pemigewasset already connects Rivergreen to the base area of the projected expansion of Loon to South Mountain. Apparently the mountain is moving to the town. Just more Yankee ingenuity at work.

MOUNT WASHINGTON SKI VALLEY

Below the great white dome of Mount Washington, New England's highest peak, is a bustling valley with towns of varying age and origin, divers accommodations, and sports facilities of every description. This is a grand playground with a half-century tradition of winter recreation.

The Skiing

Four distinctly different lift-served alpine ski resorts rise out of the Mount Washington valley. Just opposite the eastern side of the mountain is **Wildcat**, well-named and well-known for its combination of windy cold weather and traditionally-cut tricky, narrow trails. With 2,100 feet of vertical, it is the tallest of the four. It's also the most demanding, both because of the steepness and unevenness of the terrain, and because of the double fall line of the trails. Intermediates with a taste for excitement may do well on Wildcat, but novices will struggle a bit, if they attempt terrain above the simpler slopes at the bottom. No one takes this mountain for granted.

Wildcat still has its antique two-passenger gondola which provides service not only to downhillers, but to cross country skiers daring enough to drop 11 miles from its summit to the heart of the town of Jackson. The snowmaking at Wildcat has improved over time, extending now to most of the mountain, but New England veterans shouldn't have misgivings; rocks, stumps, and bumps still provide excitement. The view across the valley to Tuckerman's Ravine and Mt. Washington's peak is one of the best in Eastern skiing.

South of Mt. Washington is **Attitash**, somewhat shorter than Wildcat (1,750 vertical) but still imposing. Its trails, cut in the late '60s, follow the fall line and are primarily intermediate and gentle expert runs. Its snowmaking system has been the most comprehensive and reliable in the valley.

Above the town of Jackson is **Black Mountain**, with a vertical of 1,100 feet, one chair and three t-bars. This secluded ski area dates back to the '30s, when the Whitney family put up a rope tow behind their inn. Some of its trails have been widened and snowmaking added. Whitney's Inn is bigger, too. Modern improvements are penetrating slowly, but not too conspicuously, thank you.

In the southern corner of the valley, at the eastern edge of North Conway is **Mt. Cranmore**, famous for its role in the history of skiing: Hannes Schneider, the dean of Austrian ski instructors; the ski trains of the 1930s; and the "snowmobile" lift composed of small cars on a wooden track, all Cranmore contributions to the sport. In celebration of its golden anniversary, Cranmore, with 1500 ft. of vertical, is building new lifts and improving snowmaking over its gentle broad terrain.

Each spring, **Tuckerman's Ravine** and Mt. Washington's Headwall are open to adventurous skiers. The hike into the canyon can take three hours or more. And then you start climbing. The slopes are truly steep, exceeding 45 degrees at points. Skiing the Headwall commemorates skiing's more arduous past.

Resort Life

The northern end of the valley, towards Jackson is rural, traditional, aesthetically pleasing, and seductive to outdoors people. The south, near North Conway, is by contrast urban and hectic. Good for shoppers.

Nordic Village and The Wentworth are in or near the town of Jackson.

Mountain Statistics:	Vertical	Hourly Uphill Lift Capacity	Skiing Terrain
Attitash:	1,750 feet	6,100 skiers	220 acres.
Black Mountain:	1,100 feet	2,900 skiers	16 trails
Mt. Cranmore:	1,167 feet	4,800 skiers	185 acres
Wildcat:	2,100 feet	8,600 skiers	20 miles of trails

NORDIC VILLAGE

JACKSON, NH

The downhill skiers in the group pack the car with skis, boots, poles, extra sweaters, dry mittens and lunch, and they're off to ski Wildcat. What will we do without them for the day?

We need groceries for dinner. But they took the car! No problem. With cross country skis and a backpack, we're going shopping. The Nordic Village groomed trail connects to Jackson's nationally-known 145 kilometer cross country trail network. Jackson is only three quiet miles away on the trail and we'll have a chance to poke around

in the village. We'll buy lunch and stop for a picnic on the way home. The Club House swimming pool, steam room and spa will be waiting for us.

Hungry skiers will eat anything, even healthy food, so we'll put a chicken in the oven and make a big salad. While dinner cooks, we'll take our skates down to the pond and skate on genuine outdoor, weather-made ice.

Although we are only three miles from town, we have a hundred acre wooded outpost in which to play. The Nordic Village sports activities, including cross country (a.k.a. Nordic) skiing, outdoor skating, and the hot spa, are as Nordic as the names of the buildings – Arlberg, Entelback, Bartensburg – all a reference to the fact that Nordic skiing had its beginning in the United States here in New Hampshire.

It is kind of good to be without the car. North Conway is a mere eight miles south of Nordic Village. This town has more "factory retail outlets" for clothes and household items than we knew to exist anywhere. Suppress that idea. We also have to pass up for the day a chance to play tennis on the five indoor courts of the Mt. Cranmore Racquet Club or to train on the elaborate exercise equipment of the Club.

When our downhill skiers have battled their way back to us, we'll have dinner ready, a fire in the fireplace and the bathtub jacuzzi ready for a weary skier. The apartments at Nordic Village are large enough to permit the group to engage in separate quiet evening activities without interrupting each other. We never stay up late on ski vacations. There is tomorrow to think about, and someone else will have the pleasure of going shopping with the backpack.

WENTWORTH RESORT HOTEL

JACKSON, NH

You should look this good when you're 100 years old. The elegantly renovated Wentworth, formerly a summer-only grand hotel, is now the charming centerpiece of a rethought and reorganized year-round resort. In the 1880's, when the Mount Washington Valley was discovered as a summer alternative to the steamy, crowded seaside cities, resort hotels were built to provide upper-class lodging to month-long visitors. Times changed, vacation patterns changed, and skiing changed the valley to a four season playground. The Wentworth changed too.

The Wentworth golf course now shares its 160 acres with 64 condominium townhouses built around the perimeter, designed to agree aesthetically with the classic Queen Anne style of the old hotel. The effect is not unlike a mother duck accompanied by a clutch of matching off-spring. In winter, the golf course becomes a cross country trail head, a part of the 145 kilometer Jackson Ski Touring Trail which loops through meadow, forest and village. For the condominium residents, nordic skiing is as close as the back door.

The cross country trails around the Wentworth are maintained by the Jackson Ski Touring Foundation. Half of the trails are ungroomed to appeal to back-country enthusiasts. The network permits skiers to go from Jackson to the base of the downhill areas of the Valley. Most exciting is the trip up to Wildcat, a gondola ride to the top, and an eleven-mile return from the Wildcat summit to the town of Jackson. That is cross country skiing.

The hotel is the social center for the Wentworth village-within-a-village. After-ski relaxing can be conducted among the ferns and polished brass in the hotel lounge and a little later you can have a proper white tablecloth dinner in The Plum restaurant. If you are serious about not cooking at all during your vacation, you may participate in the hotel meal plan, including breakfast and dinner. If you are serious about having a lovely meal served to you without lifting a finger or leaving the room, you can have a Plum Room dinner delivered to your townhouse.

The townhouses are large, comfortable, luxurious, and well-designed. The owners choose the furnishings and interior design, to a rigorous management standard: the apartments are different one from another, but similar in that economy appears not to have been a determining principle. The living room fireplaces are brick from floor to ceiling, the living and dining rooms have window seats for quiet reading, and the kitchens contain most known appliances.

On a sunny afternoon, take the horse-drawn sleigh ride around the grounds, with lap rugs tucked around your legs and a half-dozen half-remembered sleigh ride songs buzzing in your head. Just beyond the front of the hotel is the Jackson village square, bounded by The Wentworth, the First Congregational Church and the village library. Here in this classic New England town, with its companionable mix of Colonial, Arts and Crafts, and Shingle-style architecture, everything you do seems as though you are contributing to some life-size Christmas card. Jingle bells, jingle all the way. Oh what fun it is . . .

SUNDAY RIVER SKI RESORT

BETHEL, ME

In five short years, Sunday River evolved from a regional day center into the largest small area in New England. Located in western Maine, an hour and a half north of Portland, it now attracts more skiers each season than any other resort in either Maine or New Hampshire. The key to Sunday River's appeal is an unrelenting commitment to snowmaking, yielding the most reliable conditions in eastern New England, especially early and late in the season.

The Skiing

Sunday River forms a bowl with sides rising up to five separate peaks (others await development), the highest having a very respectable vertical of 1,850 feet. Although the runs are not especially long, this predominately intermediate area has good balance and terrain of all sorts, other than scary steeps or extended bumps. In 1988, Sunday River created the "steepest, longest, widest, lift-served trail in the East," 3,550 feet long, 200 feet wide, a pitch of 31 degrees for 60 percent of its distance and 23 degrees for the balance, served by its own new fixed-grip quad chair. The mountain has four quad chairs (one detachable) and seven other lifts, providing a remarkable hourly up-hill lift capacity of nearly 20,000 skiers per hour.

Resort Life

Sunday River has completed over 600 condominiums, in seven separate clusters, distributed in a horseshoe shape around the South Ridge base area. Tomorrow, there may be more, and by next year another 100 certainly. As recently as 1978, none existed; no lodging was available at the mountain.

Sunday River Condominiums

The condominiums have the true New England skier spirit, with attention paid to function rather

than frills. The furniture is presentable, comfortable, and durable, nothing fancy-dancy.

The kitchens are equipped sufficiently to make a sensible dinner after a hard day skiing, probably no escargot forks. And perhaps no dishwasher, which carries simplicity a mite far to our thinking.

The presumption, however, is that you've come to ski Sunday River and Sunday River expects to wow you with the quality of the snowmaking, the

new high speed lifts and no lift lines, rather than adorable upholstery. And, after all, the skier's most basic human after-ski needs – for some bubbling hot water to sit in and some cold beer to drink – are treated with respect. All condominium clusters have access to indoor and outdoor swimming pools and hot tubs. Several good bars in the base areas cater to the skier's axiomatic socialization instincts.

Sunday River's growth has brought rebirth to the surrounding communities, particularly the lovely nineteenth century village of Bethel, just six miles away. The two contrast nicely, Bethel sweetly genteel, a relic of the past, with Sunday River efficiently utilitarian, a promise of the future.

Sunday River and Bethel, three and a half hours from Boston, are a powerful combination, a contemporary ski resort with a traditional old New England town.

Mountain Statistics: Vertical, 1,854; Hourly Uphill Lift Cap., 19,550; Skiing Terrain 54 trails, 400 acres.

SKI WINDHAM

WINDHAM, NY

This is a small resort by national standards. The town of Windham is attractive and unpretentious, half a lived-in working village and half an evolving family vacation community. Main Street, neither preserved nor gentrified, fulfills its traditional role. Gentle Catskill mountains and pasture land, working farms and stone walls surround the town. Ski Windham rises on the southern side.

The Skiing

The mountain has a 1,600 foot vertical over a distance of 5,300 feet, a solid intermediate pitch. Several short drops at the top of the mountain are steep and usually bump-covered, a brief challenge to expert skiers. The balance of the mountain is intermediate cruising terrain, with novice slopes on the skirts at either side at the bottom. The adventurous novice-intermediate should try Wraparound, a two mile route down from the top.

Windham has an elaborate and excellent ski school program for both children and adults. Students can take a 12-week course meeting once or twice a day on Saturdays or Sundays. A student,

child or adult, stays with his same class for the entire period. The rates are less than they would be on a straight hourly rate. The Smokey Bear Ski School teaches children 4 to 7 years old. For children younger than that, a nursery is available at the mountain.

Well-managed snowmaking covers 97 percent of the mountain. Windham conducts both adult and kid racing programs, and has a coin-operated course for practice between events. Ski Windham's lift lines are less long than its two and a half hour drive from New York might suggest.

Resort Life

The Catskill mountains communities, once defined as summer only, are acquiring a second life as year-round resorts. Hunter Mountain, ten miles south, established the winter season in this area. Windham, downright tranquil by comparison, is similarly experiencing a mini-boom, with nice restaurants, antiques shops and art galleries adding to its appreciable natural resources.

Windham Ridge Club

The balcony of each two-story townhouse overlooks the village of Windham, with a panoramic view of the Catskill Mountains and the trails on Ski Windham across the narrow valley. A picture window beside the big fireplace supplies the same view from a comfortable chair. The apartments are furnished simply and pleasantly by their owners to a rigorous management standard.

On a crown of the hill is the large Fitness Center, containing three indoor tennis courts, a swimming pool and group hot tub. The second floor will soon become a large restaurant for the Club. Below the rows of townhouses, a golf course is being carved out of the forest.

We admit to a fondness for tennis after a day of skiing. The contrasts are so intense: from outdoors to inside, from a white world to a colorful one, from heavy clothes to light, from long-johns to tennis shorts. We like the weight change, from ten pound ski boots to sneakers weighing ounces.

Few resorts in the ski world even have indoor tennis courts, fewer still offer upper level instruction. Windham Ridge Club has both, an All American Sports Tennis Academy, with a comprehensive year-round teaching program.

Ski Windham combined with Windham Ridge Club is an ideal iffy weather choice. If the weather behaves, ski and play tennis after. If the weather disintegrates, your tennis will only improve.

We also recommend the Ski Windham-Windham Ridge duo for those just learning the sports. Ski Windham has a strong ski school. The All American Sports Tennis Academy at Windham Ridge emphasizes tennis fundamentals. And if you're already a strong downhill skier and good tennis player, you can take up teleskiing at Windham. We did.

Mountain Statistics: Vertical, 1,600; Hourly Uphill Lift Cap., 8,000; Skiing Terrain, 215 acres, 30 trails.

WHITEFACE RESORT

LAKE PLACID, NY

Which Eastern mountain has the largest vertical drop, 3216 feet? Which US mountain twice hosted the Winter Olympics? And which major Eastern mountain's lift pass is a "best buy?" We bet nine out of ten active skiers couldn't answer Whiteface after being asked all three questions. It is a sad story, but true; Whiteface is still a secret. So what is going on?

The Skiing

The skiing is challenging and diverse, as you would expect from a mountain this size. The top chair, with a vertical of 1,800 feet alone, is one of the steepest in the East. When these trails bump up, the level of difficulty equals Stowe or Bear Mountain at Killington. The middle chair has some intermediate runs with good fall lines and some cruisers that twist and turn. The bottom is flat, with a well-segregated novice area. Sounds good, is good.

Its obscurity derives, not from an absence of good terrain, but from troublesome snow conditions. Annual natural snowfall is less than neighboring Vermont's. Of late, ORDA, the Olympic Regional Development Authority has assumed management of the mountain from the State of New York. Ninety percent of the terrain is now covered by snowmaking; snow cover is much improved.

Being relatively little-known, Whiteface has only occasional lift lines on Saturdays and holiday weekends. The rest of the time, the mountain is uncrowded. On the top lift, lines are a rarity anytime.

Resort Life

Whiteface is 10 miles from the village of Lake Placid, the host community of the 1932 and 1980 Winter Olympics. The region contains facilities for every form of winter sport in Olympic competition, including such standards as skating and cross country, but also ski jumping, tobogganing, moun-

taineering, bobsledding, lugeing, and speed skating. Some are not always open to the general public, but you can, for example, take a supervised bobsled run. The Olympic Arena in Lake Placid hosts skating competitions and hockey games.

Unlike its age-mate, Sun Valley, which became a fashionable resort and playground of movie stars, Lake Placid developed into the nursery and training camp of champion athletes, who honed their skills and made their reputations here. The 1932 Olympics left a faint residue of carriage-trade establishments, but the true character of the village is unpretentious.

Whiteface Resort and Country Club

Whiteface Resort looks across Lake Placid to Whiteface Mountain nine miles north. On 360 acres next to the lake are several dozen classic Adirondack cabins, clustered around an excellent restaurant and cross country center. Thirty modern comfortable vacation apartments, to be 60 in 1992, have been added to this year-round resort.

The condominiums combine Lake Placid's straightforward functionalism with spacious interiors, attractively decorated. Balconies adjoin each apartment's living-dining area, whose broad windows share the view of mountain in the distance.

Mountain Statistics: Vertical, 3,216; Hourly Uphill Lift Cap, 7,850; Skiing Terrain 16.6 miles of trails.

CUTTLE'S TREMBLANT CLUB

MONT-TREMBLANT, QUEBEC

Mont-Tremblant is at the northern end of a valley of small villages and mini-communities like the Auberge Cuttle's Tremblant Club or Gray Rocks. The area remains rustic, in fact on the north side of Tremblant begins the endless Quebec wilderness. Resort life centers on the mini-community in which you reside.

The Skiing

This is the giant of the Laurentians, a mountain with 2,131 feet of vertical. Lowell Thomas and his sort were skiing Tremblant as far back as the 1930s. The Tremblant mythology derives from its narrow, twisting trails, cut to challenge the telemarking downhillers who cruised these runs in those early days on wooden skis without edges.

Most of the trails, therefore, are not steep--steep was unskiable in those days. With modern equipment, snowmaking and grooming, expert terrain has eroded into intermediate terrain, abundant at Tremblant. One fearsome run, Expo, tumbling down the north side of Tremblant with a true fall line, is allowed to bump up. Expo is a prime example of a modern expert challenge.

Tremblant's annual snowfall is average for the East, about 150 inches. Its snowmaking system expands each year and now covers more than 50 percent of its terrain. Lift lines can be a problem at Tremblant. Although the mountain may seem a long way away to some of us, it is only 90 minutes from Montreal, the home of a lot of enthusiastic skiers.

Cuttle's Tremblant Club

The Tremblant Club began as a small family-run inn (auberge), on a wonderful site on the shore of Lake Tremblant, directly across from the white trails that twist down the face of Tremblant. For thirty years the Cuttle's Tremblant Club's distinction has been supported by its award-winning French restaurant with the enviable view. The chef's calibre is demonstrated weekly at Thursday night's buffet.

The earlier quiet ambiance of the inn has been transformed by the construction since 1985 of eight Austrian-style chalets, each containing ten apartment suites. A European feeling is suggested by the steep roof lines, the Tyrolean embellishments, and the private balconies with the incredible view of the lake and mountains beyond. Inside, the apartments have full kitchens, one or two bedrooms, and perhaps a loft. A large raised-hearth fireplace occupies the corner of the wood-panelled living room.

Skiers staying in the apartments may choose *ad hoc* between their own kitchen and that of the inn, and between their own living room and the pleasant fire-lit social rooms of the inn. The piano bar next to the dining room in the inn encourages adult camaraderie; the nearby playroom brings children together. In 1989, the Tremblant Club will unveil a new health club with an indoor pool, hot tub and exercise facilities.

The Club has its own ski school which teaches on Mont-Tremblant. Skiers may select a vacation package including lodging in the apartments, Mont-Tremblant lift tickets, 18 hours of instruction and supervised skiing, video critique, ski movies, fondue and a few drinks as well. The Tremblant

Club staff is completely bi-lingual, which is in itself a little daunting, but you may still order dinner in French.

The Tremblant Club uses its ski school to create a social program for the week. Guests in the school see a ski training movie upon arrival Sunday night, attend a complimentary cocktail party on Monday, a fondue party on Wednesday, and an awards ceremony and video tape review on Thursdays. As important as any single event is

bringing guests together for a week of both vigorous activity and social exchange. The condominium has returned full circle to the dynamic of the inn.

Some guests will choose to get away by themselves. For these guests, the communities around Tremblant have put together a groomed cross country trail network covering 60 miles that snakes through the towns and other inns of the area. Stop at a store, glide through the woods, cross a lake, it all sounds like a great adventure to us.

GRAY ROCKS

ST. JOVITE, QUEBEC

Voltaire, reflecting France's lack of interest in North American, dismissed New France as "quelques arpents de neige" (a few acres of snow). Despite this indifference, 80% of the population of Quebec are francophone, the survivors of the undervalued empire that once covered half the continent. The Quebecois culture, language, cuisine – and joie de vivre – are alive

and well in the dozen ski villages of the Laurentian Mountains, northeast of Montreal.

The large Gray Rocks Inn, on its own Lac Ouimet four miles from Mt. Tremblant, built its considerable reputation on the instructional ski week, lessons twice a day and a party every night, room and board included. First rate instruction on every level, from beginner to master racer, takes place on Sugar Peak, the small, intensely developed mountain across the road, "quelques arpents de neige."

The ski week program bears the stamp of French-Canadian energy and stamina. Skiers join a class for six days of lessons, molding themselves together as a group for instruction, free ·skiing, even lunch. On the final day, the mountain is all but obscured by numbers of ski class races taking place, beginner through expert.

In the early part of the season, expert skiers come to Gray Rocks to tune-up for trips to the West or to Europe. Later in the year, the classes are filled by families with skiers of all abilities. The collective enthusiasm from within the classes carries over to life in the Inn. The dining room buzzes with talk. A good day on the slopes brings energy back to the Inn in the afternoon, where play continues.

The Inn has an indoor pool, exercise training center, and health spa. There is cross country skiing around and across the lake and on the adjoining golf courses. A playroom and gameroom keeps the kids entertained as long as the adults keep supplying the quarters.

The Village des Soleils

Success begets success, which here begets a health spa, and controlled expansion. The Village des Soleil vacation apartments were built by Gray

Rocks for a reason almost two thousand years old: there was no room at the Inn.

The Village apartments add a new aspect to the Gray Rocks experience, a range of choices. Eat with your class in the dining room or with your family or friends in the apartment. Swim or work out with a trainer at the Spa, dance in the bar at the Inn, or sit around your fireplace at home. Children can use the Inn's game rooms or snare you into a game of Monopoly after dinner. The many public rooms of the Inn are an extension of your private apartment.

For Americans, skiing in Quebec is a trip abroad without leaving US time zones, a ski trip to a French-speaking country where US money is pleasantly powerful and where American enthusiasm and candor are appreciated and matched. France did less with half a continent than Gray Rocks has done with these "few acres of snow."

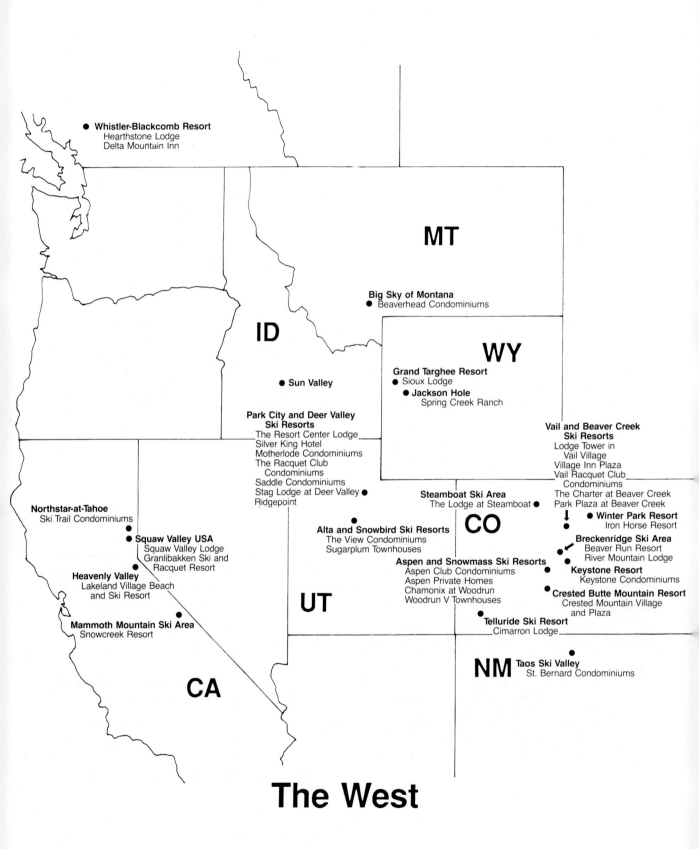

Whistler-Blackcomb Resort
Hearthstone Lodge
Delta Mountain Inn

MT

ID

Big Sky of Montana
● Beaverhead Condominiums

WY

● **Sun Valley**

Grand Targhee Resort
● Sioux Lodge
● **Jackson Hole**
Spring Creek Ranch

**Park City and Deer Valley
Ski Resorts**
The Resort Center Lodge
Silver King Hotel
Motherlode Condominiums
The Racquet Club
Condominiums
Saddle Condominiums
Stag Lodge at Deer Valley ●
Ridgepoint

**Vail and Beaver Creek
Ski Resorts**
Lodge Tower in
Vail Village
Village Inn Plaza
Vail Racquet Club
Condominiums
The Charter at Beaver Creek
Park Plaza at Beaver Creek

Steamboat Ski Area
The Lodge at Steamboat ●

Northstar-at-Tahoe
Ski Trail Condominiums

● **Squaw Valley USA**
Squaw Valley Lodge
Granlibakken Ski and
Racquet Resort

CO

● **Winter Park Resort**
Iron Horse Resort

Alta and Snowbird Ski Resorts
The View Condominiums
Sugarplum Townhouses

Breckenridge Ski Area
Beaver Run Resort
River Mountain Lodge

Aspen and Snowmass Ski Resorts
Aspen Club Condominiums
Aspen Private Homes
Chamonix at Woodrun
Woodrun V Townhouses

Keystone Resort
Keystone Condominiums

Heavenly Valley
Lakeland Village Beach
and Ski Resort

● **Crested Butte Mountain Resort**
Crested Mountain Village
and Plaza

UT

Mammoth Mountain Ski Area
Snowcreek Resort

Telluride Ski Resort
Cimarron Lodge

NM Taos Ski Valley
St. Bernard Condominiums

CA

The West

TAOS SKI VALLEY

The Taos Ski Valley is a tiny Alpine community nestled in steep, heavily forested mountains. Its architecture and atmosphere are European. Fifteen miles below is the desert valley of the Rio Grande and the town of Taos, dominated by Native American and Mexican history and culture. This mix of influences, the contrast between mountain and desert, and the pre-eminence of non-Anglo cultures gives visitors a feeling of being abroad. The challenge of the mountain provides further stimulus.

The Skiing

Experts will love the bump runs and the terrifying chutes on this mountain. They will find true fall line challenge on Al's Run and Snake Dance. Above Snake Dance, they can struggle in the double fall lines of Inferno and Mixing Bowl. Off the top lift on the front peak, they can drop into the very steep chutes, best skied in three feet of fresh snow. Intermediates can wander carefully around the fringes of the front mountain and freely in the back bowl where the terrain is moderate. Novices, well, they will struggle at Taos, with only a short bottom slope being suited to their talents.

But no worry. Novices, and intermediates and experts, join the ski school. Skiers at Taos are not just invited to ski school. Those staying for the week are virtually compelled to enroll, and frankly most love it. The week's package is sold with a ski school ticket. We have never been able to price accommodations without it. And Ernie Blake, Taos' founder, is firmly convinced that when much is asked of novices, and others, much will be learned. Ski school gives a social coherence to this resort in which most of the guests stay for the week and interact with other guests in the Valley.

Perhaps most surprising in this most southerly of all American major resorts is the quality of the snow. Again, altitude proves to be more important than latitude, and Taos' 9,200 foot base elevation (the lifts reach 11,819) assures both good cover and good powder in all but drought years.

Resort Life

The inns of the Ski Valley, particularly the St. Bernard, provide a European bar and bistro ambiance and are the center of after-ski life. The inns stage musical entertainment, often a folk singer or rock band. They also put on movies, lectures, and cultural events.

The town of Taos is the out-growth of a Taos-Tiwa Indian settlement nearly a thousand years old. The Taos Pueblo, built of timber and adobe several stories high, is still occupied and the surrounding Indian community flourishes. Indian art is supplemented by a Mexican and Anglo artist community.

Mountain Statistics: Vertical, 2,612 feet; Hourly Uphill Lift Capacity, 7,250 skiers; Skiing Terrain, 1,000 acres, plus.

ST. BERNARD CONDOMINIUMS

TAOS SKI VALLEY, NM

Taos Pueblo. Many of the apartments are decorated with examples of the indigenous Indian pottery and weaving. Many have rough adobe walls and rounded fireplaces.

The apartments are two-bedroom units. The living rooms and front balconies look out over the Valley at Al's Run dropping down the face of the mountain.

The St. Bernard condominiums enjoy a sibling relationship with the Hotel St. Bernard. Both are under the direction of Jean Mayer, a warm, personal presence in the dining room by night. Guests staying at the St. Bernard condominiums have the enviable privilege of joining Hotel guests for dinner. Served family style at one sitting, dinner is the social event that brings visitors together. Condominium guests may choose to buy a six or seven-day ski and meal package.

The St. Bernard is also right on the slopes and serves a full meal at lunch. In the "old days" the lifts use to close for lunch. This tradition has disappeared, but lunch is still an event.

The St. Bernard also has a hot tub, available to guests of the condominium. Together with the Hotel, this is the insider place to stay, the center of this miniature universe.

The village of Taos Ski Valley owes double debts. The design of the Hotel St. Bernard, for example, reflects the Swiss-French tradition of the former homelands of Ernie Blake, the founder of Taos Ski Valley and of Jean Mayer, the proprietor of the St. Bernard and Technical Director of the Taos Ski School. On the other hand, the design of the St. Bernard condominiums just across the small valley reflects the influence of the

This universe is easily and profitably left by those who wish a change of pace. The 900 year old Indian Pueblo is worth a visit as is the home of D.H. Lawrence. On the way to the latter, take a look at the gorge of the Rio Grande which drops an extraordinary 650 feet below the bridge which spans it.

The shops of Taos display a range of art work and jewelry, Anglo, Indian, and Mexican. Silver and turquoise bracelets and necklaces appeal to many visitors. The central square of Taos is Mexican in feeling. Its restaurants have bars in which you can find local entertainers.

On a very different note, indoor tennis can be played at the Taos Tennis Ranch, just outside Taos.

If you would prefer to stay home, the apartments provide a nice retreat. The kitchens are fully equipped to prepare meals or to engage in the alternative recreation of family cooking. The combination

of the apartment and the Hotel is attractive. Leave your skis in the Hotel locker at the base of the lift, an eight-minute walk from your apartment.

CRESTED BUTTE MOUNTAIN RESORT

CRESTED BUTTE, C0

Crested is as close to undiscovered as any major resort in the United States. Somewhat removed from Colorado's main axis, less accessible than the Summit or Vail, Crested has been put aside by many skiers, a resort to ski another day. That day has come. Together the mountain and the two villages at its base have grown into a small, first rate resort.

The Skiing

Until 1988, the mountain's terrain was mostly intermediate and novice with three good expert runs off one chair. For non-experts, the scope and quality of the runs was excellent. Then Crested put in a small poma that magically provided access to 260 acres on the North Face that previously were skied only by knowledgeable locals with the strength and inclination to climb. This addition was not a marketing ploy, but a real gain that gave the mountain balance, and increased the skiing terrain to over 800 acres.

Crested's strengths are the related conditions of good snow and an uncrowded mountain. The base of the mountain is at 9,100 feet, the peak at 11,400. Annual snowfall exceeds 300 inches. These figures in and of themselves are not striking, but because the mountain has fewer skiers than elsewhere, the snow stays fresher and untracked snow lasts a day longer than elsewhere. The absence of lift lines is not unpleasant either.

Resort Life

The village at the base of the mountain remains formless, although very serviceable. The few shops, restaurants, and accommodations have easy access to one another and to the slopes, but visitors are never quite sure they have come in the right door. Two miles below the mountain village is the old mining town of Crested Butte, a delightful, partly preserved, partly restored mountain town. A shuttle runs between the two. By all means, stay at the mountain village, but eat dinner a couple of nights in the old town.

Because of its relative remoteness, the spirit of the back-country continues at Crested. Telemarking is very much in evidence on the slopes and lessons in it are available. Snowboarding and snowshoeing are encouraged and back-country snowcat touring is a skiing option well worth considering here. Withdrawal enthusiasts should try a day or a night at the Irwin Lodge, an on-mountain hostelry accessible only by snowcat. The Lodge sleeps 22, who live and eat in communal isolation. Snowcat trips take guests to the untracked bowls of the Ruby Range.

Mountain Statistics: Vertical: 2,300 feet; Hourly Uphill Lift Capacity, 13,550; Skiing Terrain 800 acres.

CRESTED MOUNTAIN VILLAGE

CRESTED BUTTE, CO

At the base of the lifts at Crested is a small village with a base lodge, restaurants, and shops. Interwoven within these services are the apartments of Crested Mountain Village. Just below this tiny core, 200 feet or so from the lifts is the Plaza, a condominium tower with an atrium and mall in its center.

The apartments of Crested Mountain Village (a property name, not the name of the base area) are the upscale end of the village's rental apart-

ments. These penthouses above the on-slope restaurants and shops have immediate views of the slopes. The decoration is lavish. The living rooms have high ceilings raised well above the broad beam construction and long couches facing the stone fireplace centerpieces of these rooms. The bedrooms are not oversized but are also lavishly decorated and the master bathrooms have a jacuzzi and sauna. No expense is spared here.

In the neighboring Plaza tower, the apartments

are more modest. The Plaza has a multi-story atrium-like lobby. The apartments are informal, combining stucco and concrete construction and modest mountain rustic decor. Most of the 100-plus units here are two or three bedroom.

The Plaza has a swimming pool, health club and a variety of outdoor hot tubs. It also has two restaurants, the Saloon, informal, with a lounge and fireplace and the Tin Cup Cafe which serves breakfast, lunch and dinner.

Staying within this complex of the Crested Mountain Apartments or the Plaza, guests are in the center of action at the mountain. We nonetheless recommend a trip to town to the Slogar Bar and Restaurant (chicken and biscuits) or to Le Bosquet, (French) with a stop on the way home at the old Western bar, the Wooden Nickel.

TELLURIDE SKI RESORT

TELLURIDE, CO

The setting of Telluride, a Victorian mining town in a box canyon is strikingly beautiful. If you love steep runs, the beauty is compounded by the excitement of trails cascading down the front of the mountain into the town.

The Skiing

This mountain is a heaven for experts and novices. Ski terrain is spread out among three areas: the front face immediately above the town, a ridge running along the top of that face, and a long, gentle bowl set back away from the ridge. Experts, particularly those who crave bumps, will find no end of them on five trails coming down the 3,000 foot vertical front and off the top chair on the ridge.

Beyond the challenge of the face and the top of the ridge, the balance of the terrain, and there is lots of it, is quite gentle. A 10,000 foot high-speed quad and five other chairs serve long, broad trails that are ideal for novices and weak intermediates. Strong intermediates must choose between these relatively easy runs and the Plunge, now groomed and reclassified double blue — advanced intermediate. Those skiers who work hard at the beginning of the week will grow into the glories of this double blue challenge.

Telluride appropriately boasts both good snow conditions and no lift lines. The uphill capacity to beds-in-town ratio is about as favorable as any ski area around and there is no major city or even large town within daily commuting distance.

Mountain Statistics: Vertical, 3,105; Hourly Uphill Lift Capacity, 10,826; Skiing Terrain, 735 acres.

CIMARRON LODGE

TELLURIDE, CO

Telluride's accommodation are spread out between the town at the closed end of this spectacular, steep-sided box canyon and the base of the original lift up the face of the mountain, the Coonskin lift, at the open end. (Telluride is developing yet another housing choice, the Mountain Village, at the base of the ski bowl on the mountain, a ten-minute drive from town. The Mountain Village is still so small that it has few services and no after-ski life although the apartments themselves are handsome and deluxe.)

The Cimarron apartments are in the second and third stories of the base area at the Coonskin lift. A glance out the window tells you not only the snow conditions, but also the state of the lift line. (We have never seen one on Coonskin.) Ski clothing and equipment shops and informal restaurants share the ground floor arcade next to underground

parking for Cimmarron residents. A large indoor hot tub looking out over the snow-fed trout stream which runs behind the complex is reserved for the guests of Cimarron and is the social center.

The living rooms of the one and two bedroom apartments in Cimarron are small but attractively decorated, each like the other. French doors and intricate window patterns face onto the slopes. Although the kitchens are suitable for light cooking, the Telluride evening recreation is dining out. Cimarron residents cross a bridge over the stream and stroll into the old section of town for dinner. Two very attractive restaurants, Julian's in the New Sheridan Hotel, northern Italian cuisine, and La Marmotte, French, provide most conducive atmospheres for dinner. Before they return home, guests should stop in at the New Sheridan's bar. A monument to Victorian excess, its decor recalls the days of William Jennings Bryan, who is said to have given his "Cross of Gold" speech here. By the time he found Telluride, which in those days did not have an airport, you can bet he had the speech down cold.

ASPEN AND SNOWMASS SKI RESORTS

ASPEN, CO

A spen and Snowmass are in balance. Aspen is an old mining town that attracts singles and couples from the fast lane who seek excitement and night life. Its shops glitter, its restaurants are spoken of with reverence, and its bars and discos are active into the early morning.

Snowmass, 20 minutes from Aspen, in contrast, is a planned resort built in the 1960s to meet the needs of families, a residential community of private houses and condominiums located on the mountain itself. Families come here and take full advantage of the conveniences and facilities of on-slope condominiums.

The Skiing

Aspen

This contrast continues in the skiing at each resort. Aspen Mountain, one of four in the Aspen-Snowmass area, is an expert-intermediate mountain with many short steep drops interwoven with wandering intermediate trails. Most skiers stay on the top half of the mountain taking short chairs up the two primary ridges. The top of the mountain has cruising terrain.

Intermediates can use the gondola to ski the top and never even bother with the gullies and faces of the bottom.

Novices are invited to the friendly terrain of Buttermilk, on the edge of town, five minutes away by bus. This is a quiet center, and an excellent learning area, the home of the experimental Vic Braden Ski College. At Buttermilk, intermediates also can mellow out. For those who can forgo the limelight of fashionable Aspen Mountain, Aspen Highlands is only a few minutes away. Despite having the largest vertical rise in Colorado, it is all but ignored. Its topography is like Aspen Mountain's, gradual ridge runs followed by steep drop offs. Liftlines here are rare indeed and almost always avoidable through astute lift selection. Lift ticket prices are modest, particularly for families.

Snowmass

Snowmass is a broad, gentle mountain with more than twice the skiable terrain of Aspen Mountain. The mountain broadens at its summit. Lifts on the bottom right and left diverge as they rise and connect with three chairs up to three peaks. The mountain's 3,615 feet of vertical rise, the second greatest in Colorado, is attained over a distance of two and one half miles, all of it with consistent pitch. With the introduction of high speed chairs, the trip to the top is now less than 20 minutes. The terrain on this broad face is mostly intermediate. Off one summit is the famous Big Burn, a cruiser's paradise where only an occasional stand of pines breaks up the smooth, gradual, long snowfields.

On the right, the Campground chair has expert pitch and several bump runs, but the overwhelming tone of the mountain is intermediate, consistent with the family skiing appeal of the resort.

Resort Life

Aspen

After-ski action in Aspen always started at Little Nell's, but with a new hotel rising at the spot, a new center will have to be found. In the late evening, Andre's and Paragons remain the liveliest discotheques. Andre's, with its handsome Victorian interior, but very modern dance floor, evokes a craving for champagne, which if you wish to belong, we suggest you order. One of the most handsome bars in town, and one of the most popular, is the bar at the Hotel Jerome, a good meeting place at the intersection of Main and Mill Street, somewhat out of the center of action.

Perhaps Aspen's greatest appeal is the vitality of its town. Its art galleries are legion. Its shopping for clothes, gifts, jewelry, and sporting goods is comprehensive and tasteful. If you want any kind of service be it an accountant, doctor, lawyer, or more modern, an advertiser, educator, marketer, or travel advisor, just stand up in Hyman Mall and holler.

Eating out is *de rigueur* in Aspen. One restaurant or another is often described as "the best between New York and L.A.," Gordon's being the latest candidate. (How do "they" know? "They" never eat in between New York and L.A.) There is, of course, no requirement to eat French or Continental cuisine. Most other national menus are represented from Japanese to Mexican, Arabian to Vietnamese.

Alternative sports also flourish in Aspen. The Aspen Club is one of the most comprehensive sports centers in the ski world. A second tennis center is found opposite Buttermilk at the Grand Champion Club. The Ashcroft Ski Touring Center is highly recommended for the quality and aesthetics of its trails, and the food and ambiance of its restaurant. An additional network of cross country trails runs about the valley connecting Snowmass with Buttermilk.

If all of this is too much for you, join the common Aspen practice: stay up late, sleep late, and start the day about 11:30 with brunch and a Bloody Mary. If every night in Aspen is Saturday night, every day is, self-evidently, Sunday.

Snowmass

Resort life in Snowmass centers on the Village, on the right side of the mountain. Groups of condominiums and two hotels surround a small mall of shops and restaurants. After skiing the mall can be crowded and lively but at night it is quiet. Snowmass has built a large teenage center to meet the needs of this often overlooked population.

For a unique dinner (or lunch for that matter) you can dog sled into Krabloonik off the Campground chair. If you really want to get away from the kids, the final retreat might be hot-air ballooning. The kids, however, will probably want to come along.

Mountain Statistics: Aspen Mountain: Vertical, 3,267 feet; Hourly Uphill Lift Capacity, 11,575 skiers; Skiing Terrain, 625 acres. Snowmass: Vertical, 3,615 feet; Hourly Uphill Lift Capacity, 20,535 skiers; Skiing Terrain, 1,560 acres.

ASPEN CLUB CONDOMINIUMS

ASPEN, CO

The Aspen Club condominiums are located up the canyon toward Independence Pass a half mile from the town of Aspen. They fit unobtrusively into the aspens and pines of the narrow valley. The living rooms of each townhouse apartment face a small stream running down the canyon. These apartments are spacious and comfortable.

In this quiet, rustic setting, the Aspen Club has put together a facility and program that is, quite simply, quite extraordinary. The Club offers instruction and competition in racquetball, squash, wallyball, fencing, indoor cycling, free weights, volleyball and basketball. Seven days a week, it has classes in aerobics and fitness. The Club runs a swimming program, including junior and adult

training, novices-to-competitors, in its 25 yard pool, which is also available for just plain recreation. Three indoor tennis courts are the site of adult league competition, a "Superdrill" adult group lesson program, and a junior program.

As a guest for a short period, reservations are recommended for facilities such as tennis and squash. To participate in the group programs, guests upon arrival should ask for the athletic schedule, which is printed monthly.

The Aspen Club has its own cross country trail network, 3.6 miles of groomed trails, starting on the property.

The Aspen Club does not have a restaurant of its own, although there is a lounge in the Club, a center in which to relax and have a snack or a drink. The Club is affiliated with the Aspen Club Lodge, which is located right at the base of Aspen

mountain, adjacent to Aspen's top-to-bottom gondola, the Silver Queen. The Lodge has an excellent, elegant restaurant of its own.

ASPEN'S PRIVATE HOMES

ASPEN, CO

Aspen has many spectacular private homes, many huge, many equipped with every luxury and toy you might imagine and more. They are often in a setting that confers privacy, while offering dramatic views of the town and of Aspen Mountain beyond.

Red Mountain, opposite Aspen Mountain, is one of the locations of these homes. Other private houses are available in town. On Red Mountain the houses are modern. In town, they may be either modern or Victorian. They range in size from three bedroom to bigger, appropriate for large families or sharing families. While they are hardly inexpensive, when the cost is shared, they may be comparable to less dramatic housing choices.

Snowmass also has many private homes, a good rental option there. Many of the homes are located above the condominiums on the ski mountain. You can ski out your door, and come home on the lifts. Some, in fact, are a good drive up from

the base and require use of a car after the lifts close. Their sizes vary from ample to palatial.

In both Aspen and Snowmass, these homes are managed by rental agents who will provide every type of service from airport pick-up to grocery shopping. The one service that is generally not available is transportation to the mountain. If you rent on Red Mountain, you will almost certainly want at least one car.

When renting a private home put together questions which are most important to you: size, location, type of facilities – including a game room, separate television room. Try to imagine what the needs of your group will be. In the right house with the right group of people, you may enjoy a very special ski vacation.

And by the way, if you wish your rental to confer prestige, Red Mountain is the present "in" address. That is where the stars rent. Next year, the town of Aspen may be "in" or perhaps Snowmass. But the advantage of renting, rather than buying, is that when the style changes, your foundation is easily moved.

CHAMONIX

SNOWMASS, CO

The road leading to Chamonix passes under the slopes of Snowmass. Lifts rise on either side and skiers descend past its large windows.

This tall Mediterranean appearing structure in the midst of the slopes, houses 28 one and three-bedroom apartments. Elevators serve every floor from the pool to the roof. Located in the middle of the snow-covered slopes, these apartments fill with light which radiates in every window. The exterior and interior of the building is built and decorated in white stucco and light woods. The living rooms back-up to a sun room with large plate glass windows facing onto the valley below Snowmass and to the mountains beyond. The kitchens are large and colorfully decorated. Bathrooms have one and two-person jacuzzis.

Chamonix is run like a full-service hotel. Daily

maid service is standard. The staff will shop for you, before you arrive and during your stay. Common areas include a lounge with liquor service, a deck with an outdoor hot tub and swimming pool, and an exercise room. Cable television with HBO is a standard feature as are washers and dryers. Underground parking is available if by chance you bring your car. Alternatively, and preferably, Chamonix will send a car to meet you at the nearby Aspen airport if you let them know when you are arriving.

Chamonix has walking access to Snowmass Village, by paths that, like its entrance road, pass under the ski trails. Additionally at the bottom of Snowmass, well below Chamonix, is a shopping mall with a large supermarket and other stores. Chamonix will give you a ride to these services as well, but delivery is also available. When you are in the middle of the slopes, who cares to travel by any other means than skis? That is the pleasure of on-slope living in surroundings so condusive to good cheer.

WOODRUN Ⅴ TOWNHOUSES

SNOWMASS, CO

Woodrun V is located in the middle of the lower slopes of Snowmass. Built in townhouse structures, each apartment has direct access to the outdoors, an inducement we feel to rise early and get out on the skis. When the lifts start running and skiers glide below your living room windows, it is difficult not to be drawn onto the slopes.

The interior of the apartments feature huge stone fireplaces and large beam construction. The

less, Aspen is a mere 12 miles away. Buses run between Snowmass and Aspen until midnight. After that, a cab will get you home or you can wait for the free skier shuttles that run throughout the day.

If you are tired of skiing and want an exercise alternative, the Snowmass Club, a mile from the mountain, is a comprehensive athletic facility. It has indoor tennis courts, racquetball and a complete aerobics, health, and weight training center with professionals to give guidance.

For families with teenagers, the mountain, the resort village with its mall and its teen center, the supporting facilities of the resort and Woodrun V work well.

feeling of luxury here, which is real, comes from the solidness of the construction. The living space is divided into living room and dining room areas each with a view out over the slopes. The bedrooms are on the upper floors. Bathrooms in many of the apartments have two-person jacuzzis or saunas. The layout is that of a small house.

Location is one of the principal features of Woodrun V. By itself in the middle of the slope, well above the base of the lifts but at the same elevation as the mall of Snowmass Village, the activities of the mall are a two-minute walk by paths that tunnel under the slopes. As such, these apartments have seclusion, yet do not miss out on the action.

The Village does provide a choice of restaurants including a Chinese and a Mexican restaurant. The most distinguished choice for eating in Snowmass Village is Shavano's. With a pretty view over the mall and out onto the valley, Shavano's serves a menu of fresh fish, duck, steak, fettucini, salads, and homemade breads. The menu changes every night. Being in a condominium on a vacation does not require you to cook. Reservations are recommended at Shavano's.

After dinner, checkout The Brothers' Grille lounge at the Silvertree Hotel on the Mall. It often has a performer at work. After that, a short, brisk walk home will make you ready for bed.

Do not forget that at Snowmass if you get rest-

VAIL AND BEAVER CREEK SKI RESORTS

VAIL and AVON, CO

"Vail announces a major expansion." Someone should check with the Antitrust Division of the Justice Department to find out whether this is legal. We thought Vail was already the biggest ski area in America, depending, we know, on how you judge, but in a single blow it has doubled its terrain.

Then you add Beaver Creek, just down the road from Vail, developed by Vail Associates. Beaver Creek is a major resort in its own right. It has a terrific mountain and a community of elegant, luxurious homes and apartments at the base.

The Skiing

Vail

It is fair to say that Vail has it all: good steep bump terrain on Chair 10, cruising runs for skiers of all abilities throughout, novice terrain at the bottom and the *top* (including a kid's ski playground), quiet areas near Lionshead that most skiers choose to ignore, gigantic powder fields, back bowls, now bigger than ever. The distance from the top of Mongolia Bowl to the bottom of the new lift will exceed seven miles.

Vail and Beaver Creek are also located in a snow belt and are as likely to have good snow early as any resort in America. Just in case, both resorts have snowmaking on the bottom slopes that, particularly at Vail, are largely unskied except at the end of the day. Brown spots look terrible – and discourage skiers – even if we know there is snow elsewhere.

The lift system is very modern. Vail is the leader in the installation of high-speed quads. There are now six in place at Vail and more to come.

Beaver Creek

We say without qualification this is a first class mountain. It has some of the longest and best groomed cruising trails (Centennial, the downhill course for the men's World Championships in 1989), novice terrain at the top of the mountain, and long, long bump runs in the Birds of Prey area, something for everyone.

The mountain, still being developed, has 800 acres of skiing, with another 300 to come. Its vertical is a grand 3,340 feet. If or when it receives approval for expansion onto the neighboring Arrowsmith area, its vertical will expand to 4,000 feet, the greatest in Colorado and third only to Whistler-Blackcomb and Jackson Hole in North America. Trails are already cut at Arrowsmith.

Both Beaver Creek and Vail have comprehensive ski school programs. For adults, there are specialty classes: bump clinics, race classes, 6½ hour per day sessions and Sybervision workshops. For children, full day classes are available for those over 3½ years old. Rental equipment is included in the children's ski school fee. Children should also try the kid's ski playground, a new diversion in skiing.

Cross country lessons are also available, one involving a "Gourmet Tour" that breaks up the day.

Resort Life

Vail

Vail was also a leader in the development of the purpose-built mountain village. The village has spread the length of the mountain's face from the eastern-most lift to the Westin Hotel beyond Lionshead. Free shuttle buses run up and down a bus-only designated road, making transportation within Vail quick and reliable.

A community of this size supports services of every shape and size. There are three top flight athletic clubs: the Vail Racquet Club, the Vail Athletic Club, and the Cascade Club at the Westin Hotel. There is indoor skating, snowmobile tours, snowcat tours, and sleigh rides. If Vail has any weakness it may be that its groomed cross country trails are limited to nearby golf courses.

Restaurants are too numerous and diverse to list, but let us start on the gourmet end with La Tour, The Left Bank, the Sonnenalp, the Wildflower Inn at the Lodge, and The Vail Racquet Club, a locals' favorite. Less formal, popular, and in the heart of Vail village are Cyrano's (Continental) and Los Amigos (Mexican) To escape from town and try something still less formal, a popular trip is to Minturn to the Saloon (Mexican) or the Country Club (Steaks). We could go on.

The center of night life is along Bridge Street at the Bridge Street Shuffle, Sheika's in the basement of Pepi's Gasthoff Gramshammer, and Cyrano's. More boisterous and outside of the village center is the Altitude Club in the Doubletree Inn.

Beaver Creek

The base area of Beaver Creek is quiet, perhaps too quiet. Within a small core complex are several restaurants, the Park Plaza condominiums, shops, and the day lodge includes a restaurant and bar that often has live music after skiing. Below and above this core have been built homes for the rich and famous and condominiums that range from expensive to very expensive. In all, the residential development is tasteful and attractive. For restaurants one should try Mirabelle or the Golden Eagle Inn in the base area or The First Season at the Charter, all serving a Continental menu. Our suggestions in Minturn provide a convenient, informal alternative. For entertainment, the lounge at the Charter or the brand new Inn at Beaver Creek, both often have quiet music. The feature of Beaver Creek night life is the sleigh ride and dinner at Beano's Cabin on the mountain. The ride starts right at the base area.

Even more exotic is a night spent at Trappers Lodge, high on the mountain. Trappers is accessible only from the lifts. It is a cabin that sleeps six guests but comes with a staff of two who serve the guest lunch, afternoon tea, a gourmet dinner, and a full breakfast. Guests are left alone in the evening to congregate in front of the fire or to take a hot tub on the deck looking out over the mountains to the Gore Range in the north and east. Tell your hosts at Trappers before you go what you want in the way of skis, food, beverage and all will be yours. We suggest a late afternoon cross country tour of the upper meadows, followed by an outdoor hot tub emersion with champagne in hand, and then a lively, fireside discussion of . . . Well, we will leave the subject matter to you.

Mountain Statistics: Vail: Vertical, 3,100 feet; Hourly Uphill Lift Capacity, 35,020 skiers; Skiing Terrain, 3,787 acres. Beaver Creek: Vertical, 3,340 feet; Hourly Uphill Lift Capacity, 15,209 skiers; Skiing terrain, 800 acres.

LODGE TOWER

VAIL, CO

The Lodge Tower was a part of the Lodge at Vail, the distinguished hotel that dates back to the first days of the resort in 1962. The Tower was built in 1973 but the apartments have been carefully renovated in recent years. The Tower is now on its own and has transformed itself into a refined condominium complex.

The Lodge Tower continues the tradition of expensive, luxurious appointment, established in its former association. Furniture is sparklingly new, substantial and traditional in style. The decor is light and bright; the current demand is for strong colors and gay interiors. That is what guests at the Lodge Tower will get.

The apartments, one, two or three bedrooms, are suites, products of their history as part of the hotel. The brand new kitchens feature all conveniences to prepare full meals quickly. For those who would prefer not to cook in the morning, the Lodge serves a complementary continental breakfast in its lounge.

Each apartment has a fireplace and a balcony that looks onto the mountain or over the village. The Tower has its own group hot tub, for relaxing or socializing after skiing. It does not have a res-taurant of its own but its location makes it but a few seconds from many of the best restaurants, formal or informal, in Vail.

The Lodge Tower is located a few feet from Vail's once revolutionary, now old-hat-at-Vail, Vista Bahn, the high speed, detachable, bubbled quad that takes skiers to mid-Vail in nine minutes. It is also a stone's throw from the center of town, yet it is backed up against the mountain away from traffic, pedestrian or otherwise. All these pluses of location are not easily achieved.

VILLAGE INN PLAZA

In December, 1962, when Vail opened for skiing, it immediately ranked third in size among United States ski areas. Two double chairs, a poma and the West's first gondola served 900 acres of skiing terrain. The newborn village of Vail consisted of a deli, a drugstore, a liquor store, a skiers' dorm, two lodges, and the Vail Village Inn.

In the intervening years, the expansion on the mountain and the growth of Vail village have been duplicated by the Vail Village Inn. The Inn has flourished, transformed over time from unpretentious to polished, from simple to anything but. This 60-room inn has become the nucleus of a lodging, dining and business complex, filling out the better part of a city block.

The first group of apartments, built in the late '70s, is connected to the Inn and shares its resources, including a large indoor group hot tub and pleasant public rooms. Adjoining the Inn is a large plaza containing a heated swimming pool and outdoor sculpture from an associated art gallery.

Across the plaza is the latest addition to the Vail Village Inn compound, a Vail Bavarian-style building with fine apartments located above several street-level businesses and restaurants. The plaza apartments front on a pedestrian walk-way, thronged with skiers bound for the Vista Bahn lift two and a half blocks away. The cosmopolitan owners (some of them famous people) decorate their apartments individually, often lavishly, always with discriminating taste.

Within this village-within-a-village are three restaurants, the continental Ambrosia, the German Alpen Rose, and the friendly American-style Pancake House. Ski rentals, ski tuning, and lift tickets are available on-site.

VAIL RACQUET CLUB

VAIL, CO

count and catalogue the exercise machines of this club. These machines come with trainers who we think are ultimately serious and knowledgeable about their function. A large aerobic room has its appropriate mirrors and sound. Swimmers, triathletes – no kidding, and just plain guests can take some laps, or relax in a 25 meter pool.

If you are threatened or exhausted by the description of these activities, be assured that the Racquet Club has developed an excellent haute cuisine restaurant, featuring, among other things, great desserts. You see the health club has a function after all. Locals from Vail frequent the Racquet Club dining room.

Location, we have said. Yes, the Racquet Club is in East Vail, off the beaten track, five miles from the mountain. Free Vail bus service at 20 minute intervals shuttles back and forth to town. For some this is decidedly a disadvantage, but for others who enjoy Vail's great mountain and a respite from Vail's vitality, the quiet of the Racquet Clubs's rural setting appeals. From the window of your apart-

The Racquet Club is a Vail landmark with an extraordinarily loyal following. It is prized for it special features and, perhaps surprisingly, for its location.

Most importantly, true to its name, it has three indoor tennis courts, racquetball and squash courts. Its health club could be an Olympic training base. It would take an olympic mathematician to

ment you see trees and mountains, not skiers.

Vail's tracked cross country trails are located two miles from the Racquet Club at the Golf Club. After a fresh snow, guest can just put on their skinny skis and glide across the flat lands of the valley to these trails. For back-country enthusiasts, the route over Vail pass begins right outside the door. Unless you are strong, you might think of getting a ride to the top of the pass and working you way back to the Racquet Club.

The Racquet Club apartments have dark wood walls and beams. They are comfortable, and well-cared-for, not a statement of fashion. But this low key style is consistent with the relaxed atmosphere of the Racquet Club. Here you are in one of America's greatest ski resorts, provided with innumerable athletic facilities, and a first class restaurant, and yet the surroundings are quiet and contemplative.

This is a setting that nourishes the development of both mind and body.

THE CHARTER

AVON, CO

I f there is a model of the Grand Hotel for the 1980s, the Charter at Beaver Creek might be that model. The scale is less grand, reflecting a recognition of the limits of nature. The ceilings are 10 to 12 feet, not 15 to 20. The flourishes of decoration are reserved. Wall-to-wall carpets have replaced runners that once highlighted the hard wood floors of the old wide corridors of those earlier hotels.

Despite its relatively smaller scale, nothing about the Charter is little. It boasts an impressive 156 bedrooms or apartments, some the size of hotel rooms, but most two, three and four bedroom units. The architecture is conservatively modern.

The decoration of the apartments varies with the taste of each owner, but have no fear, each apartment is handsomely appointed. The apartments all have fireplaces, fully equipped kitchens, and washers and dryers.

Like a grand hotel of past ages, the Charter projects a feeling of solidity. This is a substantial institution, built to last. As you walk the corridors and get lost looking for the multi-story underground garage, the health club, one or another restaurant, or the lobby, the Charter's size impresses itself upon you.

Once you find your way around, you will be pleased with what is offered. The health club has a large pool, a masseuse, a hot tub, weights and an exercise room. Children will be amused by activities in the game room. Two restaurants, the Terrace, casual, the First Season, formal, provide guests with an eating choice as well as social center and bar.

The Charter is about 300 yards from the lifts, and closer still to a trail coming off the mountain. For those who dislike walking in boots, Beaver Creek has shuttle service.

PARK PLAZA

AVON, CO

Park Plaza is a stunning, post-modern five story condotel within the base area at Beaver Creek. The base complex consists of a conference center, day lodge, a few shops and restaurants, plus this very handsome residence.

Park Plaza was built in 1985 as a full service condotel. The lobby of Park Plaza is a large, comfortable space, a social center for the guests of Park Plaza. A free continental breakfast is served here daily and on Tuesday nights guests come together for cocktails compliments of Park Plaza. A balcony off the lobby looks over the Plaza's indoor pool, making swimming a part of the life of the complex. Off the pool, is a large jacuzzi, and beyond that an exercise room. Adjoining the

lobby are ski lockers for each apartment in a room with a "skier's door," a door that is light-activated and opens to the outdoors. There is no fumbling with skis and poles here.

The apartments at Park Plaza are mostly two bedrooms. Both bedrooms are elaborate, each with a bath area that is open to the bedroom and has a large two-person tiled whirlpool. Some of the units have a third bedroom. The living rooms are elaborately decorated in pinks and greens. French doors with multi-pane windows open onto balconies that face the slopes of the mountain or down into the valley. These doors are mirrored by interior doors setting off closets. Furnishings are plush.

Park Plaza does not have its own restaurant, but the Golden Eagle Inn and Mirabelles, both Continental and good, are right across the walkway in front of Park Plaza. Not in the village, but of particular note is Beano's Cabin on the mountain. Beano's is a private club by day, and an elegant restaurant by night accessible only by sleigh. The evening's excursion is recommended.

KEYSTONE RESORT

KEYSTONE, CO

Keystone built a community from the ground up. Under the supervision of one corporation, it developed the mountain, designed and constructed a resort village, and integrated many sets of condominiums into the overall plan.

It now operates this community meticulously, seeing to every detail of service. Its care is intended to free the resort guest from any concerns about daily needs and direct his attention to the pleasures of a week of sport and relaxation.

The Skiing

Keystone Resort now encompasses two mountains, one Keystone, the second, Arapahoe Basin, 10 minutes up the road. Keystone is a small mountain by Colorado standards with a vertical of 2,340 feet. The front of the mountain is overwhelmingly intermediate. The trails are carefully groomed. Connected with the front face is North Peak, the expert area of Keystone. Nothing on North Peak is very steep. An advanced intermediate will not be uncomfortable here, except perhaps on the one or two runs that are allowed to bump up.

A-Basin is a striking contrast. With a base elevation of 10,780 feet, and a summit of 12,450 feet, much of the skiing is above the tree line on broad, steep faces. Several of the trails in the wooded areas of the bottom chairs are tough, and two or three drops in the Pallavicini bowl area are terrifying. Do not fall here. Because of its elevation, A-Basin has the longest season in Colorado, opening in mid-November and closing in June.

Keystone is part of the Ski the Summit program, sharing a lift ticket with Breckenridge and Copper Mountain. There is frequent bus service among these areas, and the contrast among them gives the Summit a great variety of skiing. One added note: Keystone has night skiing with the largest lighted area in the West.

Resort Life

Keystone's village is built around a quarter-mile skating pond. The restaurants, shops, the Keystone Lodge and adjoining condominiums face onto this brightly lighted area with the mountain in the background. Situated on the peripheries of this center, are the many condominiums most in a wooded setting. All condominiums are run from a single reception center.

Two restaurants demand attention: the handsome Garden Room at the Keystone Lodge, and the Keystone Ranch, outside the resort, both worth the trip.

Mountain Statistics: (Keystone) Vertical, 2,340 feet; Uphill Hourly Lift Capacity, 13,400 skiers; Skiing Terrain, 680 acres.

KEYSTONE CONDOMINIUMS

Keystone's condominiums are all run by the resort itself with an iron hand that assures the preservation of the resort's hard-earned, coveted Mobil five star, and AAA four diamond rating.

The resort company has divided the condominiums into deluxe, premium, and standard units. No matter what their designation, each apartment, each piece of furniture and equipment in each apartment is reviewed by the resort and catalogued as to the date of introduction and the number of days of use. (Thank God for computers) Evidence of wear, or just plain age provokes a prompt replacement of the item in question. Standard or not, each apartment is immaculate.

Apartments of each category are located in three different sites: the resort village, the mountain base, or wooded locations within a three to five-minute bus transfer to the village or the mountain.

The Chateau d'Mont is one of Keystone's deluxe apartment complexes. These apartments are at the mountain. The living rooms have cathedral ceilings and hot tubs from which the mountain can be viewed.

No matter what the category or the location, each cluster of apartments has its own swimming pool and whirlpool, or in the case of village apartments, access to the Keystone Lodge pool and health club complex.

At the Keystone Resort, they answer the telephone by saying "Keystone," not just because it is their name, but because in the local language, the word "Keystone" means "may I help you?" Not a bad question.

BRECKENRIDGE SKI AREA

Breckenridge is in the heart of the Summit area which includes the resorts of Keystone-Arapahoe Basin and Copper Mountain. Of these resorts, Breckenridge alone has a town, and a lively one at that. The old wooden Victorian buildings have been refurbished and painted in bright colors with highlighted trim. There is a frivolity to the shops of Main Street. The town makes you want to play, but that is why you're there.

The Skiing

The skiing covers a huge expanse of 1,500 acres on three peaks, named for their geological map designations as Peaks 8, 9 and 10. Novices will love much of this terrain, particularly on the long bottom of Peak 9 and the lower reaches of Peak 8. Intermediates will be equally pleased by the extent of suitable terrain. Experts must hunt and pick and still will face inevitable run outs. At the top of Peak 8 they will find bowl skiing off a poma lift. On the north face of 9 is some good woods skiing. And on the extreme left of Peak 10 there is a steep run with three sharp drops, ideal for powder, but the return to the lifts from the bottom of these drops takes a little work.

Breckenridge is very high with lifts rising above 12,000 feet. It does receive less snow than neighboring Copper or Vail, about 250 inches a year. Despite the certainty of snow at top elevations, the mountain has installed a major snowmaking system thus insuring consistent cover by creating an early season snow base.

Resort Life

The town of Breckenridge is fun. It starts with a history and continues with an enthusiasm which it passes on easily to its guests. The little shops and multi-story old wooden buildings which have been transformed into malls with mixed uses draw vacationers in. A cafe may be next door to a game room. A camera store and ski shop share a floor with a gallery.

The resort's size supports a broad assortment of restaurants from haute cuisine, (Spensers at Beaver Run) Mexican, (Mi Casa), to informal, (Gator) or steak (Ore Bucket Lodge). For lunch at the foot of Peak 9, Quigley's has an attractive soup, salad, and croissant menu.

Health club and sports facilities are associated with particular lodges or condominiums. Cross country skiing is available at two centers, the Nordic Ski Center and Whatley Ranch.

Breckenridge, both its town, and its skiing, is good for families in which the kids – and the parents – are mature enough to wander about on their own.

Mountain Statistics: Vertical, 2,610; Hourly Uphill Lift Capacity, 22,650; Skiing Terrain, 1,500 acres.

BEAVER RUN

BRECKENRIDGE, CO

Beaver Run is in all respects a full service condotel. If in your imagination you can turn the snow of the slopes of Breckenridge, which adjoin Beaver Run, into water, you might think of it as a huge cruise ship with all of the resources you will need for a week and then some.

The accommodations here include choices from studios to four bedroom apartments. Each has a full kitchen, many, but not all, have fireplaces. All have cable television.

Comprehensive supporting services are found throughout the five building complex. First, there is a choice of restaurants. Spencer's offers excellent Continental cuisine in a formal setting. Copper Tops has a burger and salad menu. G.B. Watson's is both a general store and a deli.

The on-premise night life is found at Tiffany's. Here you can dance to disco music and simultaneously watch yourself or a movie on a wall-projected big-as-life video.

The two swimming pools and seven supporting hot tubs, both indoor and out, extend from a large

glass enclosure out onto an open deck. Across the walkway from the pool complex is an indoor miniature golf course which will amuse a child of any age.

Because of its size, structure and full staff, Beaver Run handles groups well and easily. Its convention hall seats 1,000 people. We are not privy to its staff rooms, but we have seen this resort throw a party for 500 or so of someone's best friends. The party was elegantly presented, the food was great, and whoever it was had good looking friends, something that even Beaver Run cannot guarantee.

Beaver Run also provides shuttle service down to town, a three-minute drive away. If you get caught up in the cruise ship mentality, you may feel a need to go shopping. We can't explain just why. A better thought would be just to jump overboard onto Breckenridge's ocean of trails. You won't get wet, and climbing back on board could not be easier. At Beaver Run, all that is lacking is snow in the lobby so that it could be a ski-thru, rather than just a ski-in, ski-out resort.

RIVER MOUNTAIN LODGE

BRECKENRIDGE, CO

You will warm to River Mountain Lodge as you enter the lobby. The lobby has the feeling of an old private club with a fireplace in the corner, and large upholstered chairs and sofas around the walls and in the center of the room. Traditional lamps afford reading lights in the darkened interior and wall sconces and mirrors provide decoration. The lounge is a place for reading, for meeting, or in the evening, for listening to quiet musical entertainment with a drink in hand.

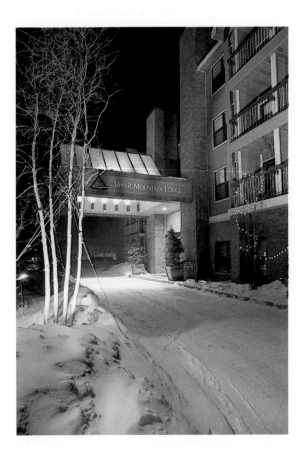

A second social center is the health club. It has an indoor hot tub, weight room and an aerobics room. An outdoor hot tub is located out on a deck overlooking the stream which runs behind the Lodge.

The apartments, in contrast to the Lounge, are modern both in architecture and in concept. Mostly studios and one bedrooms (some two bedrooms or studio lofts), they are sharply neat, bright and efficient with small fireplaces and compact kitchens.

River Mountain is located but a few steps from Breckenridge's 129 year old Main Street. Cross the small stream in back and you are in the heart of the galleries and shops of the town. Out the front door, perhaps a seven-minute walk away, are the bottom lifts of Peak 9. The town shuttle runs to the mountain every ten minutes. A ski trail, 4 O'Clock Run, returns from the mountain to within a hundred feet of River Mountain Lodge.

The Lodge does have heated underground parking, although a car is by no means essential.

When staying here you are in the middle of the Summit County area. A trip to Copper Mountain, one of the most balanced in Colorado, or to Keystone, is recommended. In fact, it is only 30 minutes to Vail, another resort of some stature. Public transportation within the Summit area is frequent and easy. Service to Vail can be arranged through the Lodge.

River Mountain, although it appears to be a condotel, does not have its own restaurant. So much the better. Within five minutes there is a choice of 20 restaurants ranging from American steak and fish to Mexican. It does serve liquor in its lounge and often has live entertainment.

WINTER PARK RESORT

WINTER PARK, CO

I n Colorado, Winter Park is a favorite. It has more Colorado residents' skier days than any other resort. Outside Colorado, despite its history and the quality of the skiing, this resort is little known. Winter Park will celebrate its 50th anniversary in 1990. It has the third largest uphill lift capacity in Colorado and complete diversity of ski terrain. The base elevation of 9,000 feet guarantees good snow. The fundamentals are all here.

The Skiing

The resort offers skiing on three interconnected mountains. The first developed, Winter Park, has terrain for intermediates and novices. The second, Mary Jane, is rightfully famous for its bump runs which come in all degrees of steepness and which are unrelenting. The third, newly developed, Vasques Ridge, is small but adds cruising terrain to the other mountains. In addition, in the right snow conditions, the mountain has snowcat skiing in back bowls.

The vertical here is only 2,220 feet, short for Colorado, but otherwise Winter Park is a big area with good fall line skiing. It also boasts a state-of-the-art 32,200 square foot children's-center right on the slope with teaching programs structured for specific age groups, ages 3-4, 5-7, and 8-13.

Because of its proximity to Denver, Winter Park can be crowded on weekends, but during the week, lift lines are a rarity.

Mountain Statistics: Vertical, 2,220 feet; Hourly Uphill Lift Capacity, 26,000 skiers; Skiing terrain, 1,325 acres.

IRON HORSE RESORT

WINTER PARK, CO

The name of this condotel is a reference to Winter Park's history as a rail-served mountain village. The 6.2 mile Moffat tunnel burrows under the Continental Divide, over 12,000 feet high at this point in the Rockies. The train stops right at the base of the ski mountain, almost at the door of the Iron Horse.

The shacks of the old town of Winter Park in which the rail construction crews lived have disap-

peared, replaced by this modern condotel which provides guests with a full range of services. Start with a health club that has weights, bicycles, saunas, a steam room, an indoor-outdoor pool, and four outdoor hot tubs. Add to that racquetball courts.

Iron Horse has a lounge and an informal restaurant, Rails, which serves a Continental menu with a salad bar. It also offers a large breakfast.

The 126 apartments of Iron Horse are located in four tall structures. The apartments are primarily studios and one bedrooms with a scattering of two bedroom units, some with lofts. Each apartment has a fireplace and a balcony facing out onto the woods surrounding the buildings. Each has a full kitchen, all equipped with microwave ovens, and many have bathrooms with private jacuzzis in them. The apartments, contemporary in design, are decorated by their owners with the help and gentle guidance of management.

Iron Horse does have some entertainment in its lounge and next door at the base area of Winter Park there may be additional entertainment at the Tavern at the Vintage. The center of evening activity is down in the town of Winter Park two miles below the mountain. Here you can rock and roll at the Stampede, or take in folk music at Fred & Sophies. The town is very lively on weekends, but generally quiet during the week.

STEAMBOAT SKI AREA

STEAMBOAT SPRINGS, CO

T his is the home of the cowboy, of Billy Kidd, and of one of the premier kids-ski-free programs in the United States. It is also a massive mountain with a very modern lift and lift line information system. The image is casual and fun, and the resort meets its image.

The Skiing

Steamboat's vertical, 3,600 feet, is the third greatest in Colorado, and only 15 feet less than number 2, Snowmass. It also has a mammoth 2,500 acres of skiing terrain, about four times that of Aspen Mountain and greater than Vail's, if you knock-off the back bowls. Its location, about four hours from Denver by car, keeps day visitors to a minimum. Add to this that at every lift there is a light board indicating the waiting time of lift lines at other lifts, and you're almost guaranteed uninterrupted skiing.

Skiers of all abilities are well served at Steamboat. Novices can have fun up top, where they should be, in the Sunshine area. Intermediates can take on all but a few double diamond runs. Steamboat occasionally suffers from an excess of grooming, but keep looking, there will be bumps somewhere. In fresh snow, the mountain is rightly known for its excellent glade skiing. Nothing here will terrify, but otherwise there is an abundance of terrain.

Mountain Statistics: Vertical, 3,600 feet; Hourly uphill lift capacity, 28,730; Skiing terrain, 2,500 acres.

THE LODGE AT STEAMBOAT

STEAMBOAT SPRINGS, CO

Steamboat is rightly known for its casual, Western style. It combines this style with an appeal toward families with young kids. One child 12-and-under skis free for each parent who buys a five-day or longer lift ticket. Some condominiums match this program, reducing the cost of accommodations for children.

The Lodge at Steamboat is one of the properties that has a kids- stay-free program. It is in the heart of the mountain community, a couple of hundred

yards off Gondola Square, the base of the eight-person gondola. The apartments are not high-tech but are comfortable, easy on the eyes, relaxing. The decoration is contemporary with pine walls and wood trim that softens modern construction. Large exposed beams cross the ceilings of the living rooms. These apartments are moderately priced, again consistent with the needs of families with young kids.

All apartments have a fireplace, a bathroom for each of the two or three bedrooms, and cable television with HBO. Guests come together at the one indoor and two outdoor hot tubs that look over the surrounding meadows and up to the mountain.

Associated with the Lodge are the Delany Condominiums located just off Gondola Square. These apartments are deluxe, many highly and attractively decorated to the taste of each owner. The Delany has an outdoor hot tub.

Guests of these condominiums are welcomed at the Steamboat Athletic Club which has an exercise program, swimming pool and two indoor tennis courts. Shuttle service is provided to this facility about one mile away.

Steamboat Resort Life

Steamboat has two centers, one the town of Steamboat Springs, the other the mountain community. The town, in the best Western tradition, has a broad main street centering casual bars and restaurants. An evening in town can be fun. Bring your cowboy hat.

The mountain community sprawls a bit. It has two main centers, Gondola Square and Ski Time Square. In our judgment the sprawl does some damage to the aesthetics, but within this community, there is a broad choice of restaurants, dance spots, shops, and related services. At Ski Time Square, we like Dos Amigos Mexican Restaurant and Mattie Silks Foods & Spirits (steaks, duck and a choice of 40 imported beers). At Gondola Square, The Helm (seafood and sushi) and The Inferno (Ribs and drinks) provide a balanced choice. At night for dancing, to be rowdy try the Tugboat Saloon, or to be mellow, with a chance to hear jazz, try the Conservatory Lounge.

Steamboat has developed a program of direct flights to the resort from such cities as Chicago, Dallas, Los Angeles, Minneapolis and San Francisco. Even as we write, a direct Saturday flight from New York has been added to this list. Steamboat, once difficult to reach because of its distance from Denver, is now easily accessible.

ALTA AND SNOWBIRD SKI RESORTS

LITTLE COTTONWOOD CANYON, UT

Alta and Snowbird, side-by-side at the top of a narrow, steep-sided canyon, receive as much as 700 inches of snow a year. And that's beautiful music to the powder skiers of the world.

The two resorts couldn't be more alike and more different. Alta, the Oldie Goldie, begun in 1938, has eight chair lifts on the mountain and four inns at the base. Snowbird, the brash newcomer, opened in 1970, now has a tram and seven chairs on the mountain, with four hotel and apartment structures at the base. Alta's inns are rustic and companionable. Snowbird's hotels and apartments, built of concrete, glass, and chrome, are attractive, highly efficient and somewhat impersonal.

The terrain and snow conditions at both resorts appeal to expert skiers and may terrify even them. Each resort has two bowls, and off each of the bowls are glades, steep trails, and perilous chutes.

Both resorts appeal to people who value simplicity and can appreciate, even enjoy, low-key evenings.

The Skiing

Alta is the smaller of the two with a vertical of just over 2,000 feet. Experts traverse from tops of chairs to the truly steep runs on the face, notably High Rustler, Stonecrusher, and Eagle's Nest. Intermediates will find groomed trails and bowls that are suitably entertaining. Novices are awarded one long chair at the base.

Snowbird conveys skiers by tram to the summit in eight minutes. The skiers' return is neither as easy nor as swift. The top is festooned with tricky ravines and treacherous drops. Only one route off the top is agreeable to intermediates who must be capable of negotiating a steep face or a snarly sector. Lower chairs serve bump trails of every description other than easy. Alas, Snowbird can be a struggle for skiers with moderate or lesser skills.

The quality of skiing available at Snowbird and Alta, together and separately, is the best reason we know to make the real effort required to learn to ski very well. The lessons taken, the fears overcome, the training endured all pay off in the powder and on the steeps at Alta and Snowbird.

These resorts are less than 50 minutes from downtown Salt Lake. Lift lines, a growing problem at both resorts during weekends and major ski weeks, can be avoided by skiers willing to ski the less popular trails.

Resort Life

Alta is quiet. The Alta Lodge and The Rustler both have excellent dining rooms, but don't go expecting action, unless a cut-throat game of after-dinner bridge qualifies. Snowbird has occasional lively moments in the Tram bar, a little dancing maybe, and a game room. The Cliff Lodge, a major, full-service hotel, has five restaurants, encompassing gourmet, spa-lite, Japanese, and Mexican. On the roof is a large outdoor pool and jacuzzi, and a floor below an extensive spa and exercise facility, with health and skin treatments too esoteric to override our inherent scepticism.

Mountain Statistics:
Alta: Vertical, 2,050 feet; Hourly uphill lift capacity, 8,500 skiers; Skiing terrain, unpublished.

Snowbird: Vertical, 3,100 feet; Hourly uphill lift capacity, 8,810 skiers; Skiing terrain, unpublished.

THE VIEW

ALTA, UT

Stonehenge, we were told, was built as a solar observatory. At dawn on the longest day of the year, the rising sun appears between two huge stone pillars, marking the summer solstice.

The Druids were clever, no doubt, to have figured this out, erring only by modern standards. Not many of us, these days, get up in time to witness the sun rise.

You can have your own Druidical experience at The View, after a long, hard day of skiing Snowbird or Alta. Kick off your heavy ski boots, strip off your winter clothes, and put on your bathing suit and a robe. Grab a beer and someone you're crazy about, and go down to the group hot tub as the late afternoon sky fills with color. The sinking sun catches the haze over Salt Lake City and turns it peach, then vermillion. The sun turns scarlet as it falls slowly, precisely between the massive rock outcroppings at the foot of Little Cottonwood Canyon, fifteen miles below.

The architecture of The View is ultra-modern, high-tech; from a distance the two buildings look like glass triangles. Each of the 20 apartments, high-tech themselves, enjoy a variation of that view, which includes the front face of Snowbird.

The interiors, each decorated by its owners, are casually lavish, differing from one another more in style than in luxury. The essence of the place, the sense conveyed of "we fortunate few" seems to have inflamed a common spirit of indulgence.

All the resources of the Snowbird Resort are convenient, including restaurants, shops, and an elaborate health club. If you lack a car (and if you cross their palms with gold), Snowbird's bellmen will provide transportation. A shuttlebus connects Snowbird with the inns and ski area at Alta.

You can ski down from The View to the Snowbird tram in a couple of minutes and return by way of Chip's Run, Snowbird's only intermediate descent from the summit of Hidden Peak. To ski Alta from The View, either take the shuttle bus or hike up on skis and return using cross country technique.

The ideal combination of the exceptional skiing in Little Cottonwood Canyon and the exceptional View is crowned by the glory of the sunset.

SUGARPLUM

ALTA, UT

"Skiing is the ultimate dance and the mountain always leads."

We saw this T-shirt slogan first on an ardent telemark skier at Alta, only a half mile up Little Cottonwood Canyon from the Sugarplum Townhouses. We subscribe to his attitude toward these celebrated, imposing mountains.

The mountain always leads. At Snowbird Resort, the mountain dictated the architecture to the architects. The resort repeats the steep granite walls of the canyon.

On a high ridge overlooking Snowbird, the Sugarplum Townhouses are small editions of the resort structures, bold and modern, three stories of concrete and glass.

The mountain always leads. The canyon's East-West orientation decreed the placement of the townhouses, capturing the extraordinary sunsets from the front of the apartments, dawn and the upper canyon from the other side. The living room wall is completely glass, as is the master bedroom above. The mountain walks right into the rooms.

The ground floor of each townhouse is given over to a garage, a pleasant advantage in an area celebrated for its annual snowfall. The second floor contains the living room with a large fireplace and the wall of glass. Up half a flight of stairs is the open dining room, high-tech and elegantly hard edge. Next is the kitchen, looking up the canyon and outside to the wooden hot tub on the terrace. This variety of interior levels restates the mountain's slopes and plateaus.

The master bedroom has a glorious view of the face of Snowbird and the lower canyon, with a private sitting area in front of its fireplace. Sugarplum Townhouses are decorated in the restrained elegance of modern functionalism with superb furniture, contemporary lighting, and sharp color contrasts.

In the morning, the bold mountain waits for you to ski down Blackjack to the Peruvian lift or to the mighty tram. At Snowbird, skiing is the ultimate dance.

PARK CITY SKI RESORT AND DEER VALLEY SKI RESORT

PARK CITY, UT

Park City has three major ski resorts within its city limits: Park City Resort (opened 1963), Park West (1968) and Deer Valley (1981). Park City is Everyman's: reliable snow, good mix of trails and practically no lift lines. Park West, the same virtues with no crowds, ever. Deer Valley is the high-end choice, what with ski valets, gourmet lunches, captive ski celebrities and relentless grooming.

Park City is more than a ski resort. It is the host of splashy international sports and cultural events, a corporate homebase to small, national businesses, and a bedroom community for Salt Lake City.

PARK CITY SKI AREA

The Skiing

Park City Ski Area has an expansive trail network spread over a series of ridges, which build on one another to a vertical of 3,000 feet. Most of the lifts and runs tend to be short, the trails branching off ridges with varying steepness. Intermediates and experts can companionably ski the same chairs, taking the run-ins and run-outs together, choosing different trails in the middle. Novices may go to the top of the gondola, and finding carefully-groomed broad slopes, wander about to new lifts and fresh parts of the mountain.

None of the terrain at Park City is terrifyingly steep, although experts can have a field day on Thaynes, a seven-minute chair serving two well-cut steep bump runs. They may also ski Jupiter Bowl, a huge expanse at the very top of the complex, with both glades and open areas, bliss in fresh, untracted snow.

Park City's great virtues are its reliable snow cover and its lift capacity which exceeds demand. Savvy skiers avoid the 20 minute gondola, except perhaps in the morning, and then only with a good newspaper for company. And they prudently avoid the Prospector chairs and the runs under them, the only lift lines or poor snow conditions on the mountain.

Park West, adjoining Park City, has the same topography, is never crowded, and its lift ticket is a "best buy."

While you are at Park City, go over to Little Cottonwood Canyon to ski a day or two at Alta and Snowbird, only two canyons, but an hour's drive away. The skiing at the two sets of resorts, Park City's and Little Cottonwood's, couldn't be more different.

DEER VALLEY SKI RESORT

The Skiing

Deer Valley ski resort is a combination of two mountains, the second behind and ultimately higher than the first. The lower peak, Bald Eagle, has residential villages at its top (Silver Lake Village) and its base (Snow Park). Both groupings contain outstanding vacation apartments and lodges, among the most luxurious and attractive in the ski world. Bald Mountain, the higher peak, rises 2400 feet and carries Deer Valley's limited stock of black diamond trails.

Deer Valley was planned to be the most elegant ski resort in the United States. Great thought has been given to the care, feeding, comfort and amusement of skiers.

As for the skiing, we think it's good, but not great, sound, but not spectacular. However, the story is less the terrain than what is made of it. Trails are broad and perfectly groomed, designed for cruising. Experts will search unsuccessfully for a good scary steep or troublesome bump run, but those who like cruising will be home free.

Because Deer Valley grooms all trails, it preserves its snow. Because it limits lift tickets when necessary – usually not – lift lines are unheard of and the snow doesn't wear out. At Deer Valley skiing is perceived as fun, to be made as easy as possible.

No report on Deer Valley is complete without noting that the food served in the on-mountain *cafeterias* is simply delicious and magnificently presented. We've even heard of skiers who stopped for lunch and somehow never get back to the slopes.

Resort Life

The history of the town of Park City is a good, if not always pretty, story. Avert your eyes from what follows if you've never thought to doubt the purity of your government's motives.

During the Civil War, the US Government got to thinking that the Mormons in the remote Salt Lake valley in the Utah Territory were doing perhaps too well in their self-sufficient agricultural community. So a troop of soldiers was sent into the Wasatch mountains, ostensibly to reconnoiter, actually to insure the Mormons didn't get it into their heads to declare an independent commonwealth. The army prospected for minerals, reasoning that a big strike would attract the very riff-raff the Mormons liked least, diluting their numerical superiority.

The 1868 discovery of ore-bearing quartz led to mines yielding half a billion dollars worth of silver, gold, lead and zinc. The tent and shanty town of 3,500 Scottish, English, Irish and Chinese miners was christened Park City in 1880. The prevailing interests of the miners were, let us say, strictly temporal. Presumably the Sin City in the mountains disturbed the Mormons' tranquility, but present evidence suggests it failed to lessen their convictions.

By World War I, the mines were played out and the miners were gone, leaving behind a quiet mountain village to live down, or live up to its sordid reputation. Were it not for the vision, energy and fortunes employed in the early '60s to recast Park City as a ski area, the village might have slowly declined into a ghost town.

As the successive ski resorts materialized, Park City accommodated skiers in burgeoning condominium suburbs, at first not enough and then rather too many. The delicate equilibrium between supply and demand is being restored. Deer Valley begot its own small residential clusters at the top and bottom of the front face.

Park City's Old Town never looked better. The hundred year-old Main Street is a successful blend of the gentrified exuberant Western Victorian houses with modern compatible versions of the same. A mildly raunchy residual cowboy element gives zest to a town never accused of taking itself too seriously.

The historic contest between saints and sinners is played out these days in the liquor laws, which require that you join a private club (typically $5 for two weeks, bring all your friends) or that you buy set-ups and a small bottle from the liquor closet of the restaurant and pour the drink yourself. Anyone who can understand alternate side of the street parking regulations will have no problem with these rules.

Mountain Statistics:

Park City: Vertical, 3,100 feet; Hourly Uphill Lift Capacity, 18,700 skiers; Skiing Terrain, 2,200 acres.
Park West: Vertical, 2,200 feet; Hourly Uphill Lift Capacity, 6,700 skiers; Skiing Terrain, 51 trails.
Deer Valley: Vertical, 2,200 feet; Hourly Uphill Lift Capacity, 11,500 skiers; Skiing Terrain, 50 trails.

THE RESORT CENTER LODGE

PARK CITY, UT

peanuts with a program of poleless snowplows. The plaza is the site for lift tickets, lessons and information. A three level arcade of ski, clothes, food, and sundry shops steps down from the skiers' plaza to the Resort Center's pedestrian entrance.

The restaurant beside the skating rink serves lunch outside, the weather permitting and it usually does. Other informal restaurants in the skiers' plaza, indoors and out, provide the locus of the 4

The Resort Center is both a set of condominiums and the core of the Park City Resort. If your curiosity were dormant, you could easily stay a week here with your family without venturing out to explore Old Town or any of the other sectors of Park City. The gondola rises out of your building, meaning that you could arrive at the top of the mountain without ever having been outside.

The Center supplies critical services and provisions for skiers. Most importantly for parents, just downstairs the Park City child-care center lures

o'clock after-ski carnival. The Baja Cantina in the middle level of the Resort Center serves excellent Mexican food and marguaritas. For a formal dinner, The Columbine is gracious and has a menu of light French food.

The apartments, ninety in all, some with three and four bedrooms, are located in the three buildings which form the sides of the plaza. This substantial core gives vitality to the Center even after non-resident skiers have returned to their homes about Park City.

The Resort Center apartments are handsomely appointed, with appropriate kitchen facilities for a vacationing family. Groceries and good take-out food are sold in the arcade shops.

If skiing, shopping and eating do not satisfy your activity needs, check your Resort Center map for the health club, the outdoor swimming pool and group hot tub, each a short walk through the interconnected buildings.

For further adventure without getting into your car, you can travel to Alta, Brighton, Snowbird and Solitude on downhill skis. Park City's Interconnect program, which guides skiers into the back country and to these other resorts, starts at the Resort Center.

SILVER KING HOTEL

PARK, CITY

Silver King is a premier example of that newest hybrid, a condotel. Here you have all the advantages of a hotel, such as daily maid service, a full-time front desk, a comfortable lobby with a big fireplace, as well as the freedom and comfort of a complete apartment. You will find a microwave oven in the kitchen and microwave popcorn among the other goodies in the welcome package left for your convenience.

The apartments are handsomely decorated with country pine furniture, large upholstered couches, and sophisticated fabrics and wall papers. About a third of the apartments include a raised hot tub at the far end of the living room with a view either of the mountain or the valley.

Silver King is one large structure made up of adjoining buildings with glass-dominated facades. The atrium design of the ground floor lobby includes

an open space several stories high, crossed by a pedestrian bridge. From this perch you can look down into the large indoor/outdoor swimming pool and adjacent hot tub, a relaxed social center after skiing. This center is the site of weekly wine and cheese parties that bring guests together.

Silver King is just across the street from the Park City lifts and just a few steps from the Resort Center's complex of restaurants, bars and shops. It does not have its own restaurant or grocery store, but because of this proximity, no matter. It is also about a five-minute walk from the largest and one of the best supermarkets east of Salt Lake and west of Denver, Albertson's. And for the trip to Main Street, a five-minute drive away, the free Park City Municipal bus service is there at your beckoning.

MOTHERLODE

PARK CITY, UT

Once upon a time, Main Street and, above it, Park Avenue, were the primary thoroughfares in this old mining town. Connected to one other by short, fairly steep cross streets, they continue to define the Old Town section of Park City. Over time, as Main Street and Park Avenue grew congested, the extension of Park Avenue which connects Old Town with the ski resort evolved into the main thoroughfare.

At the top of Park Avenue, where Old Town and the newer town meet, is Motherlode, a new and exuberant condominium apartment building. Architecturally, its modern lines are embellished with Western Victorian references, at home here on the border of old and new.

Motherlode has its own internal passage ways and parking structures, layers of rambling stairs, with covered porches and balconies adding interest.

The interiors of the apartments continue the

Victorian references, some with bay windows, some with etched glass. At Motherlode, more than in most rental vacation apartments, the owners' personal tastes are fully expressed. Some owners have decorated to magazine-cover quality. Others meet the rental standards with attention to detail. Yet others are pleasantly unconcerned with interior decoration, as such, and simply supply comfortable furniture suitable for a skiers' vacation house.

The apartments have two and three bedrooms, some with small lofts, and sleeping couches in the living room. After skiing, the outdoor group hot tub in the center of the buildings becomes the social hub for the complex. Motherlode is a good choice for a group.

Outside Motherlode, old meets new again. To the right is Old Town, with restaurants, saloons, dance halls, ski shops and art galleries, all yours for the stroll. You'll find Alex himself preparing fine French food in a bistro atmosphere at Alex's, half way up Main Street. Further up Main Street is the Eating Establishment, its east-facing glass front and attractive plants creating an agreeable environment for breakfast or brunch. Opposite Motherload, but on Main Street, is the Claimjumper, a steak restaurant with a Victorian dining room.

Four private clubs along Main Street, Downunder, Milletis, Poison Creek, and Shannons, express the mining, cowboy, Victorian and contemporary influences prevalent in Old Town.

Local artists and craftspeople have themselves embraced those cultural influences that define Park City's character. In galleries along Main Street and in the city's Kimball Art Center across from Motherlode, artists' work on display reinterprets the past. Metals that were mined reappear as jewelry and sculpture. The Western landscape and cowboy life are restated in oils and watercolors. Victorian stained class is echoed in modern pieces. Restored antiques reflect contemporary eclecticism.

Across Park Avenue to the left of Motherlode, maybe 500 feet, is the new Town Chair Lift, by far the easiest way up the mountain when coming from town. The lift rises across Park Avenue and goes on up to the top of Pay Day. If you're intermediate or better, you can ski home on Quit'n Time or Creole; if not, ride the lift down in style.

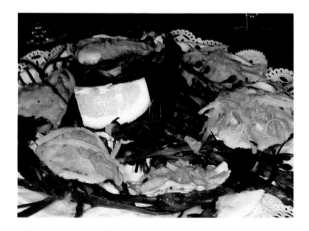

THE RACQUET CLUB CONDOMINIUMS

PARK CITY, UT

The Racquet Club apartments are a training camp for athletic fanatics who like to play three, maybe four sports a day. The only limitations are the hours in the day and the amount of sports equipment you can manage to carry along on your ski trip. Here's our personal Racquet Club intensive sports participation program.

Sport One: downhill skiing. Depart your Racquet Club apartment early for the Park City resort, either by car if you must or by the shuttle bus at the end of Racquet Club drive. Take the Ski Team chair, the best route to the top from the resort, and make your way to the Jupiter Bowl if fresh powder fell the previous night. Eat an early lunch at Mid-mountain, before the crowd arrives. Ski like a maniac until three p.m., heading down the mountain ahead of the crowd as the light gets flat.

It's time for Sport Two: tennis at the Racquet

Club, a short walk across the snow. The Park Meadow Racquet Club, as it is now called, was taken over by Park City and is open to the public. The Racquet Club is one of the best tennis facilities in the ski world, with four indoor courts, racquetball, and a large group hot tub. Park City's altitude of 6,000 feet is more favorable to good tennis than the higher base elevations of other ski resorts.

Tennis after skiing is a pleasure. You feel swift and agile in sneakers after wearing ski boots all day. The two sports reinforce each other, both requiring knees bent, weight forward. Take a quick soak in the hot tub as the stars come out over the Wasatch range.

Sport Three: cross country skiing by moonlight on the groomed trails through the golf course behind the Racquet Club. The smooth gliding movement balances the quick starts and stops of tennis.

Have a light dinner in your Racquet Club apartment and rejuvenate in front of the fireplace. These three-story townhouses, built in the late '70s, have a large living room downstairs, and an efficient kitchen facing a congenial dining area. Upstairs are two full bedrooms and a large loft.

Change into jeans and head for Old Town and Sport Four: dancing at one of Park City's clubs, perhaps Steeps-at-the-Base in the Resort Center. Don't stay out too late. Tomorrow you take it from the top again with Sport One.

THE SADDLE CONDOMINIUMS

PARK CITY, UT

From a ridge at the end of a cul-de-sac, the Saddle condominiums look across a duck pond and the Park City municipal golf course to the mountain peaks of Park City and Park West. The "saddle" between the two mountains may be clearly seen from each apartment's balcony. The Saddle apartments are conveniently half way between Park West and Park City, and economical as well.

We think a group of eight or ten reasonably well-behaved adults can have a terrific time together in this friendly environment. The kitchens are large, well-arranged, and well-equipped, so meals are easy to prepare, even for a gang. The separate dining room makes even a simple spaghetti dinner, with friendly faces glowing in the candlelight, seem like a banquet. These apartments are large: three bedroom apartments contain 2100 square feet, four bedroom apartments even more.

The apartments have saunas, steam rooms and indoor jacuzzis, evidence that they were planned for skiers, and lots of them. The furnishings were chosen by the owners to rigorous management standard. No two of them are alike, but all of them are comfortably, casually and stylishly decorated.

You'll probably want a car (or two) (or a bus) to get around conveniently from here. A garage is attached to the apartment. If a car is out of the question, or some of your skiers have different schedules, Park City obliges with a frequent free shuttle bus that stops at the end of Saddle View Road. The shuttle bus routes reliably and frequently cover the whole city, providing transportation from practically anywhere to practically anywhere else. You can get to all three ski resorts, Old Town, the grocery store and the Racquet Club from the Saddle by shuttle bus. Put your skis in the bins outside the bus, and just climb in free. Amazing.

STAG LODGE

DEER VALLEY, UT

The Stag Lodge is your basic drop-dead gorgeous. A divinely rustic, simple mountain refuge. We love the Alpine look of the buildings, the massive beams, the fieldstone fireplaces, the covered balconies, and the sunshine streaming through the windows.

The apartments are enormous: a "small" three-bedroom is 3200 square feet. The living room alone is the size of entire apartments elsewhere. The owners decorate beautifully, and presumably competitively, adopting the latest in antiques, the last word in Southwestern, the most fetching country-look linens, the best lighting, and the newest art work. The Stag Lodge is the ultimate live-in Ralph Lauren display case.

The outside is nice, too. The Stag Lodge apart-

ments are on two trails, Success (which states the case) and Last Chance (which doesn't), ski-in and ski-out. The large outdoor spa has a view of Park City, the rest of Utah, and most of North America.

Phillipe's restaurant at the Stag Lodge is lovely, decorated in forest green with Adirondack rustic chairs and antler chandeliers. The food deserves a steady high-pitched rave. You may choose to take three (or more) meals a day with Phillipe (and why not?) or you may even have your meals catered in your apartment. If you like, you can prepare your own meals in your own very fine kitchen, but seriously, why?

The Stag Lodge is not inexpensive, but the property is so extraordinary, the design so successful, the craftsmanship so fine, the effect so complete that you would agree this is what money's for.

RIDGEPOINT

PARK CITY, UT

Early in the morning, take your coffee out onto the sun deck and sit a while in the quiet light. From up here in Silver Lake Village, you can easily identify Mrs. Fields cookie factory, the Egyptian Theater and other Park City landmarks in the valley below. On a clear day, you can see the gondola going up and down. Beyond Park City, you can make out the trail patterns on Park West, and yet further the continuation of the Wasatch range. Back inside, pancakes are cooking and the family is stirring. Mornings on the mountain are precious and fleeting.

Ridgepoint was designed for skiing families who value the comfort of a large apartment with two

or three bedrooms. The kitchens are well-equipped. Finish breakfast, zip the children into their parkas, and find their mittens. Its time to go skiing.

Step into your skis and follow the trail across the ski bridge to the intermediate run down the front face of Deer Valley Resort. Zealous grooming produces ski conditions ideal for building confidence in developing skiers.

Ski home to Ridgepoint for a friendly family lunch, and spend a few minutes with your feet up on the sun deck. Or ski in to the renowned Cafe Mariposa in Silver Lake's mid-mountain lodge for an elegant lunch, graceful wine glasses on the table and ten pound ski boots under it. Deer Valley's fame rests in part upon the exceptional quality of its restaurants, remarkable for a ski resort. Less elaborate than the Cafe Mariposa is the Snuggery, technically a cafeteria, efficiently deliv-

ering the best cafeteria food in skiing history. A companion cafeteria, the Huggery, is in the base lodge at Snow Park.

After the lifts close, Ridgepoint's social life moves to the large outdoor hot tub. Children find each other and neighbors get acquainted in the soothing environment of steam and bubbling hot water. Conversation is comfortably predictable: where do you come from, where did you ski today, did you see anyone famous, and what restaurants have you been to?

You'll probably find a car essential, certainly if you want to go into Old Town at night for dinner or to wander around. After an evening in the metropolis of Park City, you'll be glad to return to your handsome, private, gracious apartment up on the mountain. Ridgepoint is a premier property at one of the ritziest ski resorts in North America.

BIG SKY

BIG SKY, MT

There is good news and more good news from Big Sky. On the mountain, the quality of skiing has improved, changed by the addition of new terrain. And the resort is largely unchanged, remaining a comfortable, secluded, sedate mountain retreat.

The Skiing

For years, we have wished for Big Sky some seriously difficult expert runs. Much of the Lone Mountain's terrain under the main lifts (two four-person gondolas) rises so gradually that it is demanding only to novices. Intermediates get long easy cruising runs, but little challenge. Now Big Sky has developed the back side of Andesite Mountain, to the left of Lone, creating a long steep slope

divided into several runs. On these steeps grow a profusion of bumps, a drawing card for experts.

This addition permitted management to groom the front side of Andesite, once the only expert area, and reclassify it as challenging intermediate. As a result, Big Sky's skiing is more balanced and much improved, although it continues to be paradise for novice and lower intermediate skiers.

Big Sky gets high marks both for abundance of snow, averaging 400 inches a year, and for an absence of lift lines. The local bed-base, as it's called, is sparse and there is no major city nearby dispensing day-trippers. The second gondola, used only weekends and vacation weeks, further guarantees no waiting.

Resort Life

"Big Sky" and "Lone Mountain" convey images of solitude and serenity. Although the mountain village has a three story commercial building (read "mall"), and although lodges and condominiums have spread from this center, the feeling of open country, of being away, remains strong here in the southwest corner of Montana. The resort supplies the surrounding region with after-ski and night life. In the mall are two restaurants with lively bars. Whiskey Jacks has a spacious dining room, a large dance floor, an ornate bar and a reputation for action. The Caboose, a small basement hideaway, often features musicians, single or in small bands.

The Huntley Lodge dining room serves an excellent Continental menu and an elaborate buffet breakfast. At night, some of the ski instructors double as Tyrolean entertainers.

The Meadow, a residential area five miles below the resort on the access road, has an outstanding restaurant, Furst Place, offering a sophisticated menu, including Western game cuisine, great desserts and a good wine list. In the canyon, six miles below the mountain, is Buck's T-4 Lodge, a genuine Montana roadhouse, serving Creole food roadhouse style. Upon request, some restaurants off the mountain will provide transportation for diners staying at the resort.

The beauty of the surrounding mountains inspires cross country skiers using the elaborate 47 mile trail system out of The Lone Mountain Ranch, four miles below the mountain base. The vast wilderness of Yellowstone National Park, etched by a network of cross country trails, is only an hour away.

Mountain Statistics: Vertical, 2,800 feet; Hourly Uphill Lift Capacity, 7,400 skiers; Skiing Terrain, 55 miles of trails.

BEAVERHEAD

BIG SKY, MT

We've all been told that the three most important considerations in real estate are location, location, and location. Beaverhead has all three. It is right on the slope, just above the lifts, and slightly aloof from the rest of the resort.

Seen from the outside, Beaverhead presents a pleasant although rather standard, three story wooden frame construction, projecting no hint of what will be discovered inside. Opening the door to any one of the apartments is like opening a page in a book on interior design and decoration.

The apartments are spacious and well-conceived, effectively segregating private areas from the common space. The Great Room, in an elbow shape, combines the large living room, separate

dining area and an open kitchen. Although the pattern is familiar, the execution is original. For example, a fireplace is only to be expected, but at Beaverhead, a picture window with a cushioned window seat beneath, perpendicular to the fireplace, is a fine spot to savor both the warmth and light of the fire and the view across the resort and down the valley.

    * Each apartment is decorated, decorated, decorated by its owners, each entirely dissimilar from every another save in the objective to fashion a

Owners have outfitted the kitchens for their own convenience, therefore completely. Beaverhead guests who prefer not to cook may enroll in a meal plan at the Huntley Lodge. Basic groceries are sold in the resort mall, supplemented by a grocery store five miles below in the Meadow area. Shuttle buses substitute for cars, which are not essential and something of a nuisance at Big Sky. Using convenient public transportation guests can get to and from the Meadows, the lower canyon, or even as far as Yellowstone.

luxurious personal residence. Beaverhead decorating standard is so high that only the bold can hope to aggressively compete.

    Each apartment has its own jacuzzi, for as many as five people at once. Apartments average more than 2,000 square feet, containing two or more bedrooms. At Beaverhead, the dimensions of the Montana sky are restated indoors.

    Guests may use the outdoor heated swimming pool, the skating rink, and the game room at the Huntley Lodge, a short walk (or quick ski) below Beaverhead. Cross country trails pass the Beaverhead apartments.

JACKSON HOLE

TETON VILLAGE, WY

Jackson Hole is untamed and rambunctious. At the base of the mountain is Teton Village, a rough-edged ski village. Eleven miles down the valley is Jackson, a commercial center with cowboy overtones and a motel strip. The mountain itself is very big, very demanding, even scary.

The Skiing

This is a mountain with great, long, often steep slopes and faces, a cruiser's mountain. Jackson Hole has the greatest vertical of any resort in the United States, 4,139 feet. At the top above the tree-line, Rendezvous Bowl offers magnificent views as prepayment for the steep challenges ahead. Elsewhere, numerous narrow chutes intimidate all but the extreme extremists. Off the Apres Vous and Casper Bowl chairs are many trails and wide slopes for the pleasure of capable intermediates. Novices and weak intermediates struggle a little at Jackson Hole. The former are confined to a few slopes near the base. The latter will find easy skiing in Casper Bowl, but difficult terrain between the Bowl and the bottom.

Jackson Hole is a wonderful mountain to ski in powder. The steep faces on the extreme left of the mountain in the Hoback area are perfectly pitched for deep powder. The mountain's exposure to the southeast damages the snow rapidly, so fresh powder is often fleeting, particularly in late February and beyond. When the conditions are right, however, the powder skiing at Jackson Hole compares favorably with the best helicopter skiing. By comparison, the tram ticket is a pittance.

Jackson Hole rarely has lift lines other than on the tram. A quad chair has been added to reach the top of the mountain. And Rendezvous Bowl now has its own poma, so skiers can stay in the bowl and go happily up and down like yo-yos. With a little cunning and a willingness to ski less popular chairs, skiers can entirely avoid lift lines at Jackson.

Resort Life

Part of the pleasure of Jackson Hole is the other, non-downhill outdoor activities. From the base of the mountain, cross country trails lead into Teton National Park. At Yellowstone, an hour's drive north, snowcats and snowmobiles take guests across snow-covered reaches to see the wonders of Old Faithful and ski the surrounding cross country trails. Outfitters and guides lead even inexperienced outdoorspeople through adventures within and outside the national parks.

In Teton Village, the Mangy Moose, a barn-like restaurant with a vaulted ceiling, elaborate rustic decoration and a steak house menu, functions as the social center. Its bar often presents a guitarist or other performing musician. In the town of Jackson, the Cowboy Bar and others like it, are worth a visit for the rock-country music, the Texas two-step, ruthless pool players and exotic saddle bar seats. The best restaurant in the entire valley, possibly the state, is the Granary at Spring Creek Ranch.

Mountain Statistics: Vertical, 4,139 feet; Hourly Uphill Lift Capacity, 9,700 skiers; Skiing Terrain, 3,000 acres.

SPRING CREEK RANCH

JACKSON, WY

Spring Creek Ranch is a small community with a large central structure and many one and two story log cabins. This community fits nicely onto the top of a mesa in the middle of the valley at the foot of the Tetons. From this mesa perch, one looks west and north directly at the jagged Teton peaks.

In every aspect of the resort, Spring Creek captures the simple elegance its founders intended. The log construction and the use of small buildings creates the atmosphere of a Western ranch. Many of the apartments are decorated by their owners in a Western style, with guidance by the Ranch. The apartments vary dramatically in design, from studios with fireplaces to two bedrooms with lofts. In the studios are Murphy beds which disappear during the day. All apartments have open floor plans. The kitchens are fully equipped and ready for use. Many of the apartments share the view north and west along the Teton range.

At the center of Spring Creek is its restaurant, the Granary, built on the edge of the mesa. The gourmet Continental and American game cuisine is elegantly presented in a small, candlelit dining room. The bar upstairs at the Granary is worth the trip at sunset even if you have to travel all the way from Salt Lake. Unwind here, and then go down to dinner.

An additional social center is an outside hot tub built into a rock formation. The behavior of the human bathers is closely scrutinized by the local waterfowl who make their home on an adjacent pond.

Spring Creek Ranch provides all of the services of a four star hotel including daily maid service, restaurant room service, and transportation to and from Jackson, four miles away, and Teton Village 12 miles away. For night life, go into town, but for solitude, tranquility and a stunning view, Spring Creek Ranch is the place to be.

At sunset the Teton Peaks are silhouetted against the bright western sky and the face of the range is dark. Nature's scale, observed from Spring Creek Ranch, offers inner peace.

GRAND TARGHEE

ALTA, WY

The peaks of the Grand Tetons tower over Grand Targhee, a little resort on the western edge of Wyoming. At the base of the slopes is a tiny skiers' village of four buildings. This insignificant human presence in the midst of the enormous forms of nature is thus described as "grand."

The Skiing
The story of Targhee is the story of snow. Like the Wasatch resorts of Utah, Targhee sits on the eastern edge of a desert plain. The moisture-carrying clouds cross the plain from the West. The colder temperatures of the mountains dump the moisture as snow, 500 inches or so each year, on the lightly forested slopes of Targhee. The slopes are moderately pitched, ideal for light powder and for learning to ski it. Two steep-sided ravines are suited to heavy powder. The resort grooms runs on these slopes so that intermediates and novices have no difficulty. Three quarters of Grand Targhee's runs, in fact, are intermediate. Three chairs and a rope tow serve the 2,200 foot vertical of the mountain, from a base at 8,000 feet.

The resort has snowcat skiing on thousands of acres of out-of-bounds terrain, some of it below the resort's base. The vertical on these runs can exceed 3,500 feet.

Resort Life

Grand Targhee is a winter camp for powder-loving families. The scale is intimate, the programs inclusive. In the base lodge is a cafeteria, a full restaurant, and a Western bar. Adjacent are two small, wood-framed hotels with 63 rooms. Down the slope from the base lodge is the **Sioux Lodge,** simple apartments in Southwest adobe style. The apartments are intimate, the kitchens compact, the essentials included. Each living room has a fireplace and glass doors opening onto a porch with a view of the valley below. The feeling is cozy and warm.

Each evening at Targhee brings a different activity: a welcoming wine and cheese party, then a casino night, ski movies one night, a regular movie another. Saturday is Parents' Night Out; the resort takes care of the kids. Skadi's restaurant serves an elegant dinner, the more pleasant for the setting. Downstairs is a bar, a relaxed spot in which to have a couple of drinks and listen to some quiet music. This is what vacation means.

Mountain Statistics: Vertical, 2,200 feet; Hourly Uphill Lift Capacity, 3,600 skiers; Skiing Terrain, 1,500 acres.

SUN VALLEY

KETCHUM, IDAHO

S un Valley, after 10 years of slumber, has returned to the competition. Its principal mountain, Baldy, three miles away from the village from which the resort derives its name, is one of the best ski mountains in America. In one summer, the resort company installed three high-speed detachable quads, one of which rises 3,144 feet from the base of Baldy in Warm Springs to the summit. Will the introduction of these new lifts

breathe new life into this self-described "grand dame" of American ski resorts? We'll see.

The Skiing

No matter where skiers turn on Baldy's complicated grid, broad slopes with consistent pitches and true fall lines invite them to make another turn. Experts can find challenge off almost any chair. On the north face above Warm Springs,

Limelight, covered by a million giant bumps, plunges down 2,000 vertical feet. Christmas Ridge, Exhibition and steep bowls at the top amuse and delight experts. Intermediates will need to keep their wits about them at all times, but they will be rewarded by long stretches of good cruising terrain. They may salivate while cruising the groomed slopes of Seattle Ridge. Novice need not apply. They can struggle at the very bottom of River Run or Warm Springs, but they are better advised to serve their apprenticeships on Dollar Mountain, three miles away at Sun Valley (in Sun Valley, Idaho).

Three new quads are a dramatic development. One quad replaces two old chairs from Roundhouse Restaurant to the summit, 1,350 vertical feet. The new Warm Springs quad, an extraordinary 3,144 foot vertical (a ten-minute ride), promises a full day's exhaustion in half a day of skiing. Even the most inveterate bump skiers will take a few cruising runs to break up the day when skiing this lift. The third quad, also on the Warm Springs' side, rises about half way up the mountain.

Baldy's short suit is snow. In "normal" years, the mountain receives only about 150 inches of snow; drought only exacerbates this truth. Two hundred and fifty acres of snowmaking helps and grooming keeps the cover adequate, but powder is infrequent.

Baldy has never had lift lines. Over time, the number of Sun Valley skiers has declined. Perhaps these new lifts will recall them, but the increased capacity should make up for any skier increase, keeping lines a rarity.

Resort Life

The logistics of this resort are confusing, particularly for those who have never been there. The resort has three centers: Sun Valley, the resort village, built in the late 1930s centered around the Sun Valley Lodge and the Inn, three miles from Baldy; Ketchum, an authentic town, with businesses, restaurants, and tourist accommodations; and Warm Springs, a vacation community at the base of Baldy, having condominiums, hotels and a few shops. Historically, skiers have focused on the village of Sun Valley, ignoring Ketchum (which

has tacky elements, but excellent restaurants, for example, Chez Michel), and Warm Springs. We foresee skier interest moving to Warm Springs, accelerated by the introduction of the two high speed chairs on that side of the mountain.

Most of the resort's condominium stock was produced in the '60s and '70s. The newer condominiums tend to be owner-occupied. In Warm Springs, handsome private houses provide the best rental properties for skiers.

Mountain Statistics: Vertical, 3,400 feet; Hourly Uphill Lift Capacity, 27,000 skiers; Skiing Terrain, 1,275 acres.

MAMMOTH MOUNTAIN SKI AREA

MAMMOTH LAKES, CA

To Easterners, the high Sierras of middle California have persistent sunshine, deep snow, high peaks, hot springs, mountain lakes, and Mammoth Mountain. The snow and trails are always obliging, the weather always warm, the skiers always friendly, and all the above almost too good to be true. The Easterners' image, in fact, states the case.

The Skiing

Mammoth confirms that elevation is one of the keys to good ski conditions. Like many of the major Rocky Mountain resorts, its base is at 8,000 feet and it rises to just above 11,000 feet. The bottom half of Mammoth is tree-covered with skiing on cut trails. The top half is entirely open with skiing in bowls, chutes and snowfields. The base of the ski mountain spreads out over a five mile skirt. The mountain sports 25 chairs and two gondolas.

A mountain this large has terrain of every description. In our judgment, seventy percent of the terrain is intermediate, but skiers of every level will find ample suitable terrain. The steep runs are at the summit, in bowls with concave cornice entrances, such as Cornice Bowl or Climax.

In non-drought years, Mammoth's season lasts nine months, through July 4th. As summer approaches, morning skiers go sailing in the afternoon.

Resort Life

Mammoth, the weekend area for Southern California skiers, is overlooked as a destination resort. The attention paid Mammoth is inconsistent with its size and quality, so weekdays are quieter than one might expect. The town of Mammoth Lakes, three miles from the base of the mountain, is a pleasant suburban-like village with shopping malls and lots of restaurants. Although the atmosphere is less than Alpine, all the services of a ski resort are here.

The beauty of the Mammoth area can be experienced at several cross country skiing centers. The best of these, in our judgment, is the Tamarack Lodge Resort. Its trails extend for 75 kilometers and circles a series of lakes, giving a real sense of this wilderness. The Lodge is rustic, an attractive place for a candlelight dinner. The Mammoth area has a broad diversity of other services. We note particularly that the local hot springs are a favorite of skiers.

Mountain Statistics: Vertical, 3,100 feet; Hourly Uphill Lift Capacity, 42,000 skiers; Skiing Terrain, 150 trails, bowls and slopes.

SNOWCREEK

MAMMOTH LAKES, CA

A century ago, John Muir called the peaks around Mammoth Lakes "the most beautiful mountain range in the world." He worried that the beauty of these mountains would be their ruin, that they would be overrun and spoiled by people who wouldn't see the mountains for their greed. Muir was instrumental in the creation of Yosemite National Park, just north of Mammoth Mountain. Yosemite's grandeur is duplicated in Pyramid Peak and Mammoth Mountain. Snowcreek Village inhabits a broad alpine meadow between the two.

Muir's apprehensions went unrealized. Sheer remoteness from major population centers during the early twentieth century protected the Sierras until a generation of environmentalists could grow up and take over the job themselves.

Environmentalism played a major part in the

planning of Snowcreek. Not only is the ultimate aim wildly ambitious – that some day ski lifts will rise from Snowcreek Base – but it resides on a cherished plateau. Natural creeks, home to rainbow trout and water birds, fed by snow run-off (hence the name) flow through the 350 acre property. The apartments are clustered, leaving expanses of open land that provide the residents with unobstructed views of the mountains, yet grant the wildlife some privacy.

The casually elegant apartments are well-designed for skiers on vacation, with efficient kitchens and big fieldstone fireplaces. Their owners decorate them, under close supervision by man-

agement, in keeping with the informal good-looks of the over-all design.

Snowcreek Athletic Club is the centerpiece of the village. Skiers will immediately appreciate the full basketball court, the lap pool, and the several hot tubs, but there is more: eight racquetball courts, a full schedule of aerobics, rowing machines and Nautilus, volleyball and a big game room. Californians play hard, too.

Mammoth Mountain is two miles away, as is the village of Mammoth Lakes. Two miles and a light year away from this quiet, beautiful community, half residential, half wilderness preserve.

SQUAW VALLEY USA

OLYMPIC VALLEY, CA

The news at Squaw Valley is the Squaw Valley Lodge. A first class accommodation has at last emerged in Olympic Valley. Squaw always had the essentials of a prime destination resort: challenging skiing, outdoor alternatives, and access to the broadest range of after-ski life from haute cuisine to Nevada's 24-hour casinos. But skiers struggled to find lodging at the mountain condusive to a week's stay. That problem solved, we shall now see if the resort's mid-week life starts to imitate the intensity of its weekend.

The Skiing

Challenging is a mild adjective for this 2,700 foot wall of snow. Starting at the far left with Red Dog, Olympic Lady, KT 22, and continuing across the top through Headwall, Siberia Bowl and on to Granite Chief, there is one cliff after another to fall from. Between are broad slopes and bowls, well-suited to intermediates. At the top of the 150-person super-modern tram, supplementing the 25 chairs, is a novice and lower intermediate area, short but located in the middle of the action to give these skiers a sense of belonging. The view of Lake Tahoe from this upper meadow will inspire skiers of all abilities to make perfect turns. The on-mountain restaurants at Squaw are also attractive, conducive to early and long liquid lunches.

The sunshine at Squaw is reliable, and so is the snow except during extreme droughts. Powder is less predictable. Huge downfalls are common, but often the snow is heavy, giving rise to the endearing name "Sierra cement." When weekend lift lines occur, the stronger skiers can select lifts on the basis of least delay. During the week, the place is yours.

Resort Life

Squaw is in the culturally varied North Tahoe region, encompassing Incline Village in Nevada with its casinos, the railroad town of Truckee, and North Tahoe on the lake. In Olympic Valley at the foot of the mountain are restaurants and bars in the Mall and the Squaw Valley Inn next to the tram building. The Olympic Village Inn has evening entertainment, including a weekly comedy night.

Within the North Tahoe triangle are seven cross country ski centers with a common admission ticket. If the groomed trails of the largest, Royal Gorge, were laid straight West, they would reach the Pacific Ocean, 200 miles away.

Mountain Statistics: Vertical, 2,700 feet; Hourly Uphill Lift Capacity, 39,380 skiers; Skiing Terrain, 8,300 acres.

SQUAW VALLEY LODGE

OLYMPIC VALLEY, CA

Decades ago when we first went to Squaw Valley (excuse me, Olympic Valley), we looked around at the threadbare village at the base and said, "This is it? After the Olympics, and everything?" The resort's infrastructure, lifts and base facilities have been greatly improved over the last five years and the construction of the Squaw Valley Lodge is yet another big step. So we can stop whining.

The Lodge complex consists of three (soon to be five) attractive buildings, each three stories, surrounding a swimming pool and health club. Apartments are on either side of a center hall with sky lights. Buildings are connected to one another by covered glassed walkways.

The apartments are cleverly designed, some with odd and appealing angled rooms. Studio-size apartments are ideal for a couple, studio-lofts and

one bedrooms will work with a child or two. Studios have efficiency kitchens, one bedrooms the full thing.

Apartments are decorated in bright clear colors, strong enough to counter-balance the sunshine that streams through the windows. The furniture was designed specifically for these apartments, so it looks smart and right, and works effectively. The same bright design elements are employed in the hallways and the main lobby, where cheerful banners hang from the ceiling.

The Squaw Valley Lodge is a condotel, fine apartments with full hotel services. A breakfast buffet is served in the lobby, which later in the day becomes the after-ski social center. A big fieldstone fireplace warms this contemporary room. The health club is comprehensive and high tech, both in fact and in appearance. In addition to lots of exercise machines, it has hot tubs, saunas, and steamrooms.

Skiing – we almost forgot, but you won't – starts just outside the door of the Lodge either from a gondola, or from the tram which glides over the top of the Squaw Valley Lodge.

GRANLIBAKKEN SKI AND RACQUET RESORT

TAHOE CITY, CA

Granlibakken feels as though it grew in the forest itself, like its sheltering tall pines and red firs. This intimate, small resort is an anomaly among the congregation of anonymous condominiums and motels that circle Lake Tahoe. Granlibakken is only a half mile inland from the western shore of the lake, but it is in another world, serene, self-sufficient, supremely private.

This resort enjoys a legitimate place in the history of skiing as the site for the 1932 Olympic ski-jumping tryouts. The broad slope used originally as a public ski jump and a toboggan run has become a well-used, well-loved instructional and recreational downhill ski area, served by a surface lift, free to Granlibakken guests. Granlibakken (accent the third syllable) means "hill sheltered by fir trees," and so it is. The resort rents ski equipment and a ski school gives lessons.

This quaint retreat is a fine choice for a group or family with a wide range of skiing ability. Expert skiers leave from here in the morning on Granlibakken's shuttle bus, bound for the steeps at Squaw. Intermediates may prefer to be dropped off at Alpine Meadows. Both resorts are only six miles away. Beginners report to ski school here to acquire basic skills without crowds or lift lines.

The authenticity of the determinedly low-tech ski area is repeated in the ungroomed cross country trails. This is how cross country skiing used to be. The freedom and tranquillity of the forest explain why people took up the sport in the first place. Lessons and equipment are available from the resort.

The cross country trails are an alternative to "going outside" into the lakeside traffic, a supplement to beginners' ski experience, and first choice if the weather contradicts a downhill day.

Granlibakken sends you out to play in the snow on a full breakfast, included in the room rate. The apartments, four to a building, are disbursed among the trees at the base of the ski area. A large outdoor group hot tub is next to the lobby in the main building.

Here more than elsewhere, owners' personalities are suggested by their apartments, decorated and furnished individually. The owners' abiding affection for this singular winter camp is conspicuous.

Other resorts can only try to simulate that natural, organic, homegrown quality Granlibakken comes by honestly.

NORTHSTAR-AT-TAHOE

TRUCKEE, CA

N orthstar is a family ski resort on 6,000 acres north of Lake Tahoe. Both the ski mountain and the apartment properties are managed under a single corporate umbrella. The reception building is at the foot of the access road, where guests check in, collect keys and a resort credit card, and a map. The resort plaza and the gondola to the ski area are at the top of the road, but the apartments are scattered in clusters among the woods, above the plaza,and along the golf course of this large resort.

The Skiing

Northstar's skiing is designed to meet the vacation needs of families. The actual base of the ski area is a short gondola ride up from the resort plaza. Skiers are carried up and away from the diversions of the resort plaza to a day lodge at the ski area base. In the day lodge is the ski school and a cafeteria. From this segregated basin, a family can ski together or divide up and meet again for a snack or lunch.

Chair lifts rise in tandem along the side of a

ridge to the summit of Mt. Pluto. Skiing from the summit consists of short drops from the ridge at sharp angles to the chairs, funnelling into runs that parallel the chairs, returning to the little basin at the day lodge. Except for the ridge drops, most of this terrain is intermediate and novice. Steep portions can easily be avoided.

On the backside of the mountain is a face with four expert runs served by a chair. None of these runs is terribly steep, but one or two are allowed to bump up providing experts with challenge.

Northstar has an impressive vertical of 2,200 feet with the feeling of a small, managable mountain, consistent with the resort's family-centered focus. It receives 300 inches of natural snow and has a back-up snowmaking system on the bottom two-thirds of the mountain.

Northstar's ski school has thought long and hard about teaching little kids to ski. Even among the very young, there are some children with precocious skills. For these fearless "ankle nippers", (a source of envy and humiliation for adult beginners), Northstar has an advanced class for three to five year-olds.

Resort Life

On either side of the resort plaza are shops and informal restaurants. Near the plaza, but hidden away from the general public in a outlying area, is an outdoor pool and hot tub center for residents

of the resort apartments. The Basque Club, an excellent restaurant serving Basque regional specialties, is two miles down the access road.

Ski Trail Condominiums

The condominiums at Northstar are built in clusters, tucked inconspicuously into the forest or arrayed agreeably across a hillside. We like Ski Trail group of apartments because of its location, next to a trail and above the resort plaza. The apartments are efficient, not deluxe. The living rooms, each with a small balcony, face the woods or the gondola track, which passes very close to one end of these buildings. The kitchens are fully equipped and each building has its own laundry.

Mountain Statistics: Vertical, 2,200 feet; Hourly Uphill Lift Capacity, 13,100 skiers; Skiing Terrain, 48 trails.

HEAVENLY VALLEY

SOUTH LAKE TAHOE, CA/NV

Heavenly Valley's skiers find big-time skiing neighboring big-time casinos. The mountain, an enormous ski area, absorbs skiers' attention by day. The casinos, downtown in South Tahoe, are comparably large and equally compelling by night. This is hardly the staid elegant milieu of Europe's chic gaming resorts, but brash, unabashed American gambling.

The Skiing

Heavenly claims to be America's largest ski mountain, based on its 20 square miles of terrain. With Vail's recent expansion, Heavenly may have been eclipsed, but it did not shrink. Heavenly is on the California/Nevada border, with runs flowing down two sides into these two states. Much of the terrain is intermediate, interesting to wanderers.

Experts who love a struggle can get their fill on Gunbarrel, a 1,700 foot true fall line drop to the bottom on the California side. Novices who ski the gentle slopes above Gunbarrel ride the tram or chairs down, like other sensible people.

The weather and snow at Heavenly are both very good indeed. The bottom may turn brown in late March, but the top of the mountain, where most of the skiing is done, maintains good snow cover long after skiers have turned to outdoor tennis and sailing on Lake Tahoe.

Resort Life

The latest rock stars, popular comedians, and retreaded lounge acts perform at Harrah's and other casinos. A late afternoon cruise to Lake Tahoe's Emerald Bay includes dinner and a sunset. Dinner at Chuck's Steak House includes a view over South Tahoe and the lake. The Christiania Inn serves dinner in a Tyrolean dining room for the sake of skiers seeking a more traditional atmosphere.

Sequestered from the casino life, and only a mile from the California base of Heavenly Valley, is Lakeland Village, a large condominium community on the south shore of the lake. Apartments, attractively decorated, range in size from studios to three bedrooms. Lakeland has its own outdoor pool and jacuzzi next to the main lodge. A second pool overlooks a long semi-private beach and the lake; by mid-March, sun bathers feel summer coming on.

Lakeland Village is an attractive oasis in the desert of mediocre motels and condominium developments of South Tahoe.

Mountain Statistics: Vertical, 3,550 feet; Hourly Uphill Lift Capacity, 26,500 skiers; Skiing Terrain, 20 square miles.

WHISTLER-BLACKCOMB

WHISTLER, BC

Recognition of the calibre of these giant mountains and the resort at their base, located at the edge of the Pacific Ocean in British Columbia, is at last creeping into the consciousness of skiers the world over. Whistler and Blackcomb, each has more vertical than any other ski mountain in either North or South America. They are now connected by common lifts and lift tickets, if not common ownership. At their junction is a new resort village, Whistler Village, which we expect will be the model for ski resort development to come. Skiers who take pride in having skied it all and skiers who pursue excellence must pay a visit to this new luminary. This resort may seem to be a long way away, but it's less than two hours by car from the Vancouver airport.

The two mountains share a lift ticket, but they are owned separately and compete aggressively. Skiers are the beneficiaries of this one-up-manship. In 1987, Blackcomb installed three detachable quads, revolutionizing its lift system. In 1988, Whistler replied with a 10-person standing gondola, (the newest ski lift technology, matched in North America only by a similar lift simultaneously installed at Stratton, VT). Whistler's gondola rises 3,900 feet over a distance of 16,440 feet (three miles) in 15 minutes and 15 seconds. Blackcomb, your move.

The Skiing

Whistler Village, the base area common to both mountains, is at the relatively low elevation of 2,214 feet. Blackcomb rises on the left precisely one vertical mile to 7,494 feet, and Whistler rises on the right to 7,160 feet. Whistler's original base below the Village gives it a total vertical of 5,020 feet. The first 4,000 feet of elevation on each mountain is heavily forested. To date, only a relatively narrow area is devoted to cut trails on either mountain, typical of this early stage of development. Blackcomb's trails are broad with excellent fall lines, providing good bump skiing. Whistler's trails tend to wander, a cruiser's mountain. Both are geared to experts and intermediates.

At 6,000 feet, the forest ends abruptly and each mountain opens up to broad bowls, both steep and gradual. Whistler's are the more extensive. Blackcomb has one major bowl served with a 6-minute high speed quad, and a north facing glacier served by a T-bar. We prefer Whistler's bowls for steepness and variety, and Blackcomb's trails for their fall lines. Even-handed, don't you think?

These mountains receive an annual snowfall of 450 inches. The ocean proximity produces both moderate temperatures and fog, but because of the dense tree cover of the lower four-fifths of the mountains, skiing is little deterred by weather conditions. And as a final testament to the quality of the snow cover, Blackcomb is now committed to skiing **365** days a year.

The World Cup racing circuit (or circus) comes to Whistler nearly every year. Whistler reaffirms this connection with world-class racing with a commitment to recreational racing. Dave Murray, a ten-year veteran of the Canadian National Ski Team, heads a racing camp providing three-day programs at the beginning or end of each week throughout the year. Some weeks, downhill technique is included with racing training. If you wish to join this program, check the schedule and reserve before you take your vacation. Because of the length of its season, Whistler-Blackcomb is the site of many summer racing programs run by ski schools and coaches associated with other resorts across America. Murray has his own summer racing camp, with tennis and windsurfing as sidelights. His summer program is for Juniors until mid-July, adults for the balance of that month.

Resort Life

This resort is centered on a new and growing ski village, for which planning began in the mid-1970s. Whistler, which had opened in 1965, was an established mountain with a small base area lacking major skier services. Development had been sporadic and chaotic. For five years, local and provincial authorities struggled with the idea of creating Whistler Village at the bottom of a valley formed by the confluence of Blackcomb and Whistler mountains. In the mid-'70s, even as late as 1980, the proposed site was occupied by a garbage dump. In the seven years since construction began, the village has been turned into a model pedestrian residential and commercial center: lodging for thousands of skiers, a score of restaurants, bars, and shops, a supermarket, a liquor store, and no car visible to the eye.

The restaurants range from the formal and Continental at The Delta Mountain Inn and the Nancy Greene Olympic Lodge, through steak (The Keg), Italian (Florentyna's), Japanese (Sushi Village), to informal hamburgers, soups and salads (Nasty Jack's). Similarly bars range from easy-going (Nancy's [Olympic Champion Nancy Greene] Piano Lounge), to swinging (The Beagle and Moguls).

Cross country skiing trails start right outside the village, rising above it and falling below, to circle the small lakes of the valley. Back-country enthusiasts can ski into neighboring Garibaldi Provincial Park, at the edge of Blackcomb and Whistler mountains. Heli-skiing, offered by three different companies, is yet another skiing option.

Whistler Village is served daily by rail from Vancouver, a trip of 2 1/2 hours. We recommend this scenic approach on the Canadian rails system (starting perhaps in Quebec City?). Whistler and Blackcomb, by whatever mode of transportation – are worth the journey.

Mountain Statistics: Blackcomb: Vertical, 5,280 feet; Hourly Uphill Lift Capacity, 19,050 skiers; Skiing Terrain, unpublished. Whistler: Vertical, 5,020; Hourly Uphill Lift Capacity, 18,800 skiers; Skiing Terrain, 2,148 acres.

THE HEARTHSTONE LODGE

WHISTLER, BC

The pattern for Whistler Village derives from European mountain towns that had come into being centuries before skiing began on the mountains around them. Zermatt and Avoriaz, among other European models, have successfully banned cars, creating a safe, uncrowded resort atmosphere. The plan for Whistler required that the automobile disappear so the streets would be clear for pedestrians.

Naturally-grown ski villages contain a balanced mix of lodging, restaurants, services and stores, each element integral to the whole. Whistler's plan required each block of buildings to address needs of Village residents, in addition to providing lodging

and dining. So Whistler's street-level shops include pharmacies, book stores, hardware stores, liquor stores and groceries. Grid patterns for street layout are sterile, so Whistler's walkways turn and curve.

Use of vertical space was also ordained by the master plan. The street level is dedicated to shops and services along covered sidewalks. Sub-street levels are reserved for potentially noisy activities, like night clubs, to sound-proof them. Apartments and hotel rooms are on the second and higher floors, the better to appreciate the view.

Whistler Village is laid out around two squares connected by the pedestrian walkway, the Mountain Square at the lifts and the Village Square in the village center. The Hearthstone Lodge is on one side of the Village Square, 300 yards or so from the lifts of Blackcomb and Whistler.

Designed by the award-winning Canadian architect, Arthur Erikson, the living rooms of these 21 apartments have slanted glass roofs facing the runs on Blackcomb. Balconies provide a view of passers-by down on the street and skiers up on the trails. The apartments vary in size from one to three bedrooms. All are equipped with the range of standard modern gadgetry from fireplaces to microwave ovens.

The Hearthstone is in the center of Whistler services. In the same building at street level is a grocery and a liquor store. Next door is Whistler's new convention center with a health club and racquetball facilities. Pubs and restaurants are within 100 feet.

In addition to all the athletic and entertainment activities at Whistler, a quiet pleasure is found in simply walking around the Village.

THE DELTA MOUNTAIN INN

WHISTLER, BC

The Delta Mountain Inn endears itself to us by all its contradictions. It calls itself an inn, and it's everything but a cozy, demure mountain retreat. It looks like a major hotel, but it's spirited and unpretentious. Its amenities read like an independent resort, but it's one of the anchor hotels of Whistler Village. It is an important link in a major Canadian hotel chain, but it's managed hands-on and personally, like an inn. It is perhaps best described as a condotel, built over a shopping center, surrounded by a sports center, located at the base of two ski areas, in the center of the resort village.

Think "hotel" and read "apartments." Depending upon your group size and taste for togetherness, you select your accommodation from the range of offerings, from a basic hotel room, through variations of studios to multiple bedroom suites with full kitchens. The front desk, concierge, daily maid and room services of a hotel enhance your apartment life.

The Inn has been a centerpiece of the Village since its beginning in 1982, and they have grown up together, each contributing to the other's suc-

cess. Delta Mountain Inn outgrew its original configuration by 1988 and was extensively expanded, renovated, reorganized and redecorated. The apartments are virtually brand new, and attractively decorated if not imaginatively conceived. Studios and larger apartments employ a Great Room layout, most with fireplaces, all with a balcony and a view.

The great feature of the Inn is the comprehensiveness of its services. Of course, it has its own restaurant, Twigs, as well as a modern lounge with evening music. Cars are stowed underground. An exercise room with Nautilus equipment, treadmills, bikes and indoor and outdoor whirlpools are found on the ground floor. Outside with a view of the mountain and the edge of the forest is a heated

pool. Two long wings of the building have been extended and a bubble placed inbetween to create Whistler's only indoor tennis courts. Delta Mountain has its own resident pro.

We've been led to understand that not everyone skis at a ski resort. Delta Mountain Inn defends the right of non-skiers to enjoy themselves at non-skiing adventures and is the information headquarters for these Other Activities. A mountain picnic, a sleigh ride, a trip to the water slide, a helicopter flight over the mountains are all arranged from here. (Is shopping classified as recreation or as a sport?)

If skiing in Quebec provides skiers with a French-flavored vacation, skiing at Whistler-Blackcomb is seasoned by the corresponding British affiliation. As early as 1849, the Hudson Bay Company's western headquarters was on Vancouver Island, a crown colony. The remainder of present-day British Columbia and the Yukon Territory, then collectively known as New Caledonia, were the major suppliers of pelts for Englishmen's beaver hats. Descendants of early Scottish, English and Irish settlers, with later contributions from Australia and New Zealand, give British Columbia, Whistler Village, and the Delta Mountain Inn a taste of modern Canada's imperial past.

APPENDIX

THE EAST

THE BATTLEGROUND, Rte 17, Fayston, VT 05673. (802) 496-2288. MAIL: RR 1, Waitsfield, VT 05673. RESERVATIONS: (802) 496-2288. CREDIT: VISA, MC, AE. BUILT: 1974-77. SCALE: 63 apartments. LOCATION: Wooded site with streams, 1 mile from Mad River Glen. PURCHASE: 2BR $92,000 (1100 sq ft). RENTAL: 2BR $190 and up. Some pkgs. Owner decorated, gentle mgmt standard. KITCHEN: Equipped to prepare holiday meal. Staples left for use. AMENITIES: W/D, cable TV, touch telephone in most, fireplace, firewood. SERVICES: Airport pickup, grocery shopping, fee. SUPPLIES: Grocery, 2 mi; liquor 3 mi. SKIING: 1 mi to Mad River Glen; 3 mi to Sugarbush. Car essential. AFTER SKI: Paddle tennis. SPORTS: X-c skiing. Skating. CHILDREN: Welcome. SPECIAL: Covered bridge, paddle tennis. Ski home from Mad River.

TRAILSIDE CONDOMINIUMS, Bolton Valley Access Rd, Bolton, VT 05477. (802) 434-2769. MAIL: same. RESERVATIONS: (800) 451-5025. SCALE: 1988 138 units. BUILT: 1970 (12 units), 1971-85 (96), 1988 (30). LOCATION: In ski village at base of ski area. PURCHASE: 2 BR (1050 sq ft) $125,000 up; 3 BR (1300 sq ft) $170,000 up. RENTAL: 2 BR-$185/night, 3 BR-$225/night; 2 night min. Owner decorated to rigorous mgmt std. KITCHEN: Equipped to prepare simple meal. AMENITIES: W/D coin-op in bldg, cable TV, telephone, fireplace, firewood provided. SUPPLIES: On-site grocery and liquor stores. RESTAURANTS: On-site; Fireside, Lindsay's. MAP avail.(B and D). Pizza del. to condo avail. SKIING: walk to lift; car not necessary. On-site ski rental, lockers, tuning and tickets. SPORTS: Sports Center in ski village: swimming, hot tub, sauna, exercise machines, indoor tennis. Skating. AFTER SKI: 2 cafe/bars; also bar in sports center. CHILDREN: welcome, under 5 ski free, stay free. Day care fee. SPECIAL: The kids' ski programs.

CUTTLE'S TREMBLANT CLUB, Mont-Tremblant, Quebec JOT120, Canada. Te: (819) 425-2731. MAIL: same. RESERVATIONS: same. FAX: same. CREDIT: VISA, MC, AX, ENROUTE. SCALE: 101 apartments. LOCATION: Lakeside site 4 miles from mountain. BUILT: 1985-8. PURCHASE: 2BR (1050 sq ft) $160,000 Can.; 3BR (1150 sq ft) $200,000 Can. RENTAL: 2 BR $160 Can.; 3BR $250 Can. Daily maid service. Generic furniture package. KITCHEN: Equipped to make holiday meal. AMENITIES: W/D, cable TV, touch telephone, fireplace, firewood. SUPPLIES: Grocery 1 mi; liquor 5 mi. RESTAURANTS: On-site dining room. Meal plan avail, complete MAP. SKIING: 1mi. to mountain, car desirable, shuttle available, ski lockers in lodge, on-site rentals, on-site tuning, tickets at desk. AFTER SKI: Piano bar, swimming pool in 1989, hot tub in 1989. SPORTS: X-c. Swimming '89. CHILDREN: Well-behaved welcome; stay free; under 6, ski free; game room. SPECIAL: Dining room in Inn. Tremblant Club's own dedicated ski school.

GRAY ROCKS, Route 327 N, St.Jovite, Quebec, JOT 2HO Canada. (819) 425-2771. MAIL: Bx 1000, St.Jovite, Quebec, JOT 2H0 Canada. RESERVATIONS: (819) 425-2771. CREDIT: VISA, MC, AE, DC, CB, EN ROUTE. BUILT: 1986-88. SCALE: 66 apartments, more to come. LOCATION: 1/2 mi from Gray Rocks Inn. PURCHASE: 2BR $144,000 Can. (1250 sq ft). RENTAL: 2BR $216 Can. and up. Owner decorated, generic pkg provided. Daily maid service. KITCHEN: Equipped to prepare

holiday meal. Staples left for use. AMENITIES: W/D, cable TV, touch telephone, fireplace, firewood, coffee and filters. SERVICES: Airport pickup, fee. Transportation to skiing. Grocery shopping, fee. SUPPLIES: Grocery 3 mi, liquor 3 mi. RESTAURANTS: Gray Rocks Inn, Le Chateau; meal plans avail. SKIING: 1/2 mi. Instruction inc in ski week pkgs. Car not essential. AFTER SKI: Health spa; machines, trainer, swimming pool, hot tub, lounges, bar. SPORTS: X-c skiing, skating, indoor tennis, riding, sleigh riding. CHILDREN: Welcome. Child care, fee. SPECIAL: Twice daily instruction, group spirit, Friday night dinner.

HAWK INN AND MOUNTAIN RESORT, Route 100, Plymouth, VT, 05056. (802) 672-3811. MAIL: Box 64, Plymouth, VT, 05056. FAX: (802) 672-5338. RESERVATIONS: (800) 451-4109. CREDIT: VISA, MC, AE, DC, CB. SCALE: 39 apartments in 1988; to be 51 in 1990. LOCATION: On mountain top, in 1100 acre site. Also 79 custom homes and 50 room inn. BUILT: 1978-90. PURCHASE: 2BR (1000-2000 sq ft) $180-250,000 up. 3 BR (1300-2500 sq ft) $220-350,000. RENTAL: 2 BR $280/night; 3BR $330/night. Owner decorated from selection provided by mgmt. KITCHEN: Equipped to prepare holiday meal. AMENITIES: W/D, cable TV, touch telephone, fireplace, firewood, seasonal welcome package, toiletries. SERVICES: Grocery shopping, ski shuttle, Xmas tree decorating. SUPPLIES: Grocery, 3 mi, liquor 8 mi. RESTAURANTS: The River Tavern, on-site. Meal plans avail. SKIING: 8 mi. to both Killington or Okemo. free shuttle, car desirable. Ski lockers, ski valet, XC rental on-site. AFTER SKI: The River Tavern bar. Health club swimming pool, hot tub; bathtub jacuzzi in apartments. SPORTS: XC inc equipment, skating pond with equip, swimming, riding, horse-drawn sleigh, weights, exercise room, exercise classes, sleds and toboggans. CHILDREN: Welcome. XC ski free, 12 and under stay free. Day care, fee. Game room. Holiday programs. Family charge card. SPECIAL: Secluded 1100 acre between several ski areas. The devotion of the staff to excellence.

HIGHRIDGE, Roaring Brook Road East, Killingtom, VT 05751. (802) 422-9611. MAIL: RD 1, Box 41, Killington, VT, 05751. RESERVATIONS: (800) 343-0762. CREDIT: VISA, MC, AE, DC, CB, CHOICE. SCALE: 104 units in 1988, to be 179 in 1990. LOCATION: On-mountain site, expected to be ski-in and out. PURCHASE: 2BR (1200 sq ft) $220,000 up. 3BR (1500 sq ft) $300,000 up. RENTAL: 2 BR $224/night, 3BR $309/night. Daily maid service. Generic furniture package. KITCHEN: Equipped to prepare holiday meal. AMENITIES: W/D, cable TV, touch telephone, fireplace, firewood, beverage pacs, welcome pacs. SERVICES: Shuttle to skiing, pending new lift. SUPPLIES: Grocery 1 mi, liquor 1 mi. SKIING: 1 mi to lift, free shuttle, until new lift built. Car desirable. AFTER SKI: Swimming pool, large outdoor hot tub in health club. Bathtub jacuzzis in apartments. SPORTS: Swimming. CHILDREN: Welcome. Game room, sleds and toboggans, holiday programs, teenagers' activities. Child-care, fee. SPECIAL: The outdoor hot tub at sunset.

SLOPESIDE, Jay Peak Ski Resort, Rte 242, Jay, VT 05859-9621. (802) 988-2611. MAIL: Jay Peak Ski Resort, Jay, VT 05859-9621. RESERVATIONS: USA (800) 451-4449. Canada 654-5754. FAX: (802) 988-2611. CREDIT: VISA, MC, AE. BUILT: 1987-88.

LOCATION: Trailside at the base of lifts, in ski village. SCALE: 79 aptmts. PURCHASE: 2BR (925 sq ft) $110,000 up. RENTAL: 2 BR $97 pp,pn, in pkgs incl skiing. Generic furniture pkgs. KITCHEN: Equipped to make holiday meal. AMENITIES: W/D, color TV, telephone in most, fireplace, firewood. Coffee and filters, hot beverage packs. SERVICES: Free child care, day and some evenings in designated areas. SUPPLIES: Limited supplies on-site, grocery store 4 mi, liquor store 8 mi. RESTAURANTS: On-site, Hotel Jay dining Room. Meal plan avail, inc bkft and din. Take-out or deliv. to condo avail. SKIING: Slopeside on Interstate trail. Tram, 100 feet. Car desirable but not necessary (shuttle loops through pkg lots). Ski lockers and boot dryers avail. On-site rental, tuning, lift tickets charged to room. AFTER-SKI: Bar in base lodge. SPORTS: Free inc. XC, skating, sleigh-riding. CHILDREN: Affirmatively welcome. Under 12 stay free. Under 6 ski free. Free day care. Game room, sleds and toboggans, holiday programs, children's activities, teenagers' activities. SPECIAL: Jay Peak's warm welcome to families with children.

THE LODGE AT STOWE, Mount Mansfield Resort, Rt 108, Stowe, VT 05672. (802) 253-7311. MAIL: Mount Mansfield Resort, Rt 108, stowe, VT 05672. RESERVATIONS: (800) 253-4SKI. FAX: (802) 253-8756. CREDIT: VISA, MC, AE, DC. BUILT: Late '70s. SCALE: 65 apartments, to be 200. LOCATION: Ski to Stowe's Tollhouse lift. RENTAL: 2BR $300 and up. Owner decorated, gentle mgmt standard. Daily maid service. KITCHEN: Equipped to prepare holiday meal. AMENITIES: W/D, cable TV, telephone, fireplace, firewood, toiletries. SERVICES: Airport pickup, grocery shopping, fee. SUPPLIES: Grocery 2 mi, liquor 6 m. RESTAURANT: Toll House, meal plan available. SKIING: Ski in/out at Stowe. Good pkgs. Car desirable. AFTER SKI: Health Club, fee. Lounge, bar in restaurant. SPORTS: X-c skiing, fee. Skating. CHILDREN: Welcome. Under 12 ski and stay free in special pkgs. Game room. SPECIAL: Ski-in, ski-out at Stowe. Stowe village. Alan Schonberger, the ski mime.

MOUNTAINSIDE, Sugarbush Village, Sugarbush Access Road, Warren, VT, 05674. (802) 583-3000. MAIL: Sugarbush Valley Real Estate, Box 234, Warren, VT 05674. RESERVATIONS: (800) 451-4326. CREDIT: VISA, MC, AE. BUILT: 1980. SCALE: 91 units. LOCATION: Center of ski village. PURCHASE: 2BR $127,500 up. RENTAL: 2 BR $230/night. Owner decorated from mgmt selection. KITCHEN: Equipped to prepare holiday meal. AMENITIES: W/D coin-op on-site, cable TV, telephone, fireplace, firewood. VT products welcome pkg. SUPPLIES: Deli in village, grocery 1 mi, liquor 6 mi. RESTAURANT: Chez Henri and the Phoenix in village (and others). Meal plan avail with Sugar Passport (pkg). SKIING: 5 min. walk to lift. Ski back on Out to Lunch. Car not essential. Free day shuttle. Ski lockers. Rentals, tuning, tickets available in village. Ski packages avail. Sugar Passport inc lodging, lifts, meals and Sports Center, midweek. AFTER SKI: Bar/lounges within walking distance. Swimming, hot tub at Sports Center (fee). SPORTS: XC 1 mi. Sports Center: skating, tennis, swimming, racquet ball, weights, exercise classes. In valley: snowmobiling, sleigh-riding. CHILDREN: Welcome. Under 12, stay free, under 6, ski free. Child care, fee. SPECIAL: In the village, on a ski-back trail.

NORDIC VILLAGE VACATION RESORT, Rte 16, Jackson, NH 03846. (603) 383-9101. MAIL: same. RESERVATIONS: (800) 472-5207. CREDIT: VISA, MC. BUILT: 1985-89. SCALE: 120 aptmts, to be 152. LOCATION: On 100 acres 3 mi south of Jackson, 12 mi north of North Conway, NH. PURCHASE: 2BR $155,000 (1200 sq ft). RENTAL: 2BR $160. Furniture pkg specified by mgmt. KITCHEN: Equipped to prepare family meal. AMENITIES: W/D in most, cable TV, touch telephone, fireplace, firewood. SUPPLIES: Grocery 1 mi, liquor 1 mi. SKIING: 2 mi to Black Mt, 4 mi to Attitash, 11 mi to Wildcat, 8 mi to Cranmore. Car essential. AFTER SKI: Clubhouse swimming pool, hot tub, steamroom. Roadside taverns 1 mi north and south. SPORTS: X-c skiing, skating, swimming. CHILDREN: Welcome. SPECIAL: Seclusion. Cross country trails leading to Jackson's 145 k network.

PARADISE, Sugarbush Village, Sugarbush Access Road, Warren, VT 05674. (802) 583-3000. MAIL: Sugarbush Village Real Estate, Box 234, Warren, VT 05674. RESERVATIONS: (800) 451-4326. CREDIT: VISA, MC, AE. BUILT; 1988. SCALE: 24 aptmts. LOCATION: In ski village, walk to Sports Center and lifts. PURCHASE: 2BR $145,000 up. RENTAL: 2 BR $230/night. Decorated by owner from selection offered by mgmt. KITCHEN: Equipped to prepare holiday meal. AMENITIES: Cable TV, telephone, fireplace, firewood. VT products welcome pkg. SUPPLIES: Deli in village, grocery 1 mi, liquor 6 mi. RESTAURANTS: The Phoenix, in the village. SKIING: 5 minute walk to Village Lift. Car not essential. Free village day shuttle. Ski lockers. Rentals, tuning, tickets avail in village. AFTER SKI: Paradise Penthouse on-site, lounges/bars in village. Swimming pool, hot tub in Sports Center (fee). SPORTS: X-c skiing 1 mi. Sports Center: skating, tennis, swimming, racquet ball, weights, exercise classes. In valley: snowmobiling, sleigh-riding. CHILDREN: Welcome. Under 12, stay free (non holiday), under 6, ski free. Child care, (fee). SPECIAL: Near Sports Center, village restaurants, ski lifts, but separated from the center village.

PICO RESORT HOTEL, Sherburne Pass, Rutland, VT 05701. (802) 775-1927. MAIL: Pico Reservation, Sherburne Pass, Rutland VT 05701. RESERVATIONS: (800) 225-7426. CREDIT: VISA, MC. BUILT: 1985-89. SCALE: 132 aptmts. LOCATION: In ski village, at base of slope. RENTAL: 2BR $180 up. Owner decorated from mgmt pkg. KITCHEN: Equipped to prepare holiday meal. Staples left for use. AMENITIES: Cable TV, telephone, fireplace, firewood. SUPPLIES: Grocery in building, liquor in building. RESTAURANTS: Season's on-site. SKIING: At base of slopes. Car desirable, not essential. AFTER SKI: Indoor pool in Sports Center, group hot tub. Lounge, bar on-site. SPORTS: Sports Center: tennis, racquet ball, exercise, weights. CHILDREN: Affirmatively welcome. Special programs. Child care, fee. SPECIAL: Sports center racquet sports. Compact village. Racing.

RIVERGREEN, At the Mill, Lincoln, NH 03251. (603) 745-6261. MAIL: Box 696, Lincoln, NH 03251. RESERVATIONS: (NE) (800) 654-6183, x 500. CREDIT: VISA, NC, AE. LOCATION: 1988 2 mi from mountain. With expected mountain expansion, at base of South Mountain. SCALE: 64 units in 5 story building. BUILT: 1987. PURCHASE: 2BR (1110 sq ft) $195,000 up. RENTAL: 2 BR $200/night; mid-week less. Daily maid service. Generic furniture pkg. KITCHEN: Equipped to prepare holiday meal. AMENITIES: W/D on-site, cable TV, touch telephone. SERVICES: Free shuttle to mountain. Grocery shopping fee. SUPPLIES: Grocery within complex, 1 mi liquor store. RESTAURANTS: In complex, Tavern at the Mill, Carlo's. SKIING: 2 mi by shuttle to mountain until South Mountain expansion, then walk

to, ski-back. Car desirable but not essential. Ski locker. Rentals on-site; tuning in town, lift tickets at desk. AFTER-SKI: Lobby lounge, Tavern Restaurant within complex; swimming pool, sauna, group hot tub at Mill House Inn within complex. Bathtub jacuzzis in apartments. SPORTS: On-site outdoor skating rink; X-C skiing on site, numerous trails in area. Swimming, weights, exercise room in Mill House Inn. Sleigh-riding, fee. CHILDREN: Welcome. Day care, fee. Game room. SPECIAL: Millfront Marketplace, including Rivergreen and Mill House Inn, stores and restaurants.

SMUGGLER'S NOTCH CONDOMINIUMS, Route 108, Smuggler's Notch, VT, 05464. (802) 644-8851. MAIL: same. RESERVATIONS: (800) 451-8752. FAX: (802) 644-2713. CREDIT: VISA, MC, AE. SCALE: 279 aptmts in village, to be 450 by 1995. LOCATION: Complete ski village at base of mountain. BUILT: 1964 through '95. PURCHASE: 2BR (1200 sq ft) $110,000 up. 3BR (1500 sq ft) $125,000. RENTAL: 2 BR $85/night/each, 4 persons, 3BR $76/night/each, 6 people, includes lessons and lift tickets. Owner decorated, gentle mgmt standard. KITCHEN: Equipped to prepare holiday meal. AMENITIES: W/D most, color TV most, telephone most, fireplace most, firewood. SUPPLIES: Grocery in village, beer and wine sold in village. RESTAURANTS: The Village Restaurant, Stanley's Cafe. Meal plans avail. Catering to apartments avail. SKIING: All apartments are near slope, within village. Car unnecessary. Ski lockers, tuning, rentals on-site, tickets at desk. AFTER SKI: Crown and Anchor Pub. Swimming pool. Group hot tub. Bathtub jacuzzi in some apartments. SPORTS: X-c skiing, fee. Swimming, indoor tennis, fee. Exercise room, exercise classes, fees. Riding and sleigh riding, fee. CHILDREN: Welcome. Child care, fee. Game room. Special programs. Teenage evening activities. SPECIAL: Alice's Wonderland child-care center. Winter riding.

SNOW CREEK, Inferno Road, Warren, VT 05674. (802) 583-3000. MAIL: Sugarbush Valley Real Estate, Box 234, Warren, VT 05674. RESERVATIONS: (800) 451-4326. CREDIT: VISA, MC, AE. SCALE: 115 aptmts. LOCATION: Base of Spring Fling triple chair. BUILT: 1983. PURCHASE: 2BR (1100 sq ft) $125,000 up. RENTAL: 2 BR $230/night. Owner decorated from selection provided by mgmt. KITCHEN: Equipped to prepare holiday meal. AMENITIES: W/D, cable TV, telephone, fireplace, firewood. SUPPLIES: Deli in village, grocery 1 mi, liquor 6 mi. RESTAURANTS: Chez Henri in the village, also the Phoenix; The Common Man in valley. Meal plan avail. SKIING: Ski-in, ski-out. Car useful, not essential. Free valley day shuttle. Ski lockers. Rentals, tuning, tickets avail in village. Ski packages, inc. midweek Sugar Passport avail. AFTER SKI: Cafes in village. Sports Center: swimming pool, hot tub. SPORTS: X-c skiing, 1 mi. Sports Center: skating, tennis, swimming, racquet ball, weights, exercise classes. In valley, snowmobiling, sleigh-riding. CHILDREN: Welcome. Under 12, stay free; under 6, ski free. Child care, fee. SPECIAL: ski-in, ski-out.

SOUTHFACE, Sugarbush Access Rd, Warren, VT 05674. (802 583-3000). MAIL: Sugarbush Village Real Estate, Box 234, Warren VT 05674. RESERVATIONS: (800) 451-4326. SCALE: 60 units. LOCATION: 1 mi from ski resort. BUILT: 1983-86. RENTAL: 2 BR $300/night; 3BR $340/night. Owner decorated from mgmt selection. KITCHEN: Equipped to prepare holiday meal. AMENITIES: W/D, cable TV, telephone, fireplace, firewood, VT products welcome pkg. SUPPLIES: Deli in ski village, grocery 1 mi, liquor 6 mi. RESTAURANTS: In valley. SKIING: 1 mi, free shuttle. Car not essential. Ski locker. Rentals, tuning, tickets avail in ski village. Sugar Passport, avail midweek, inc lodging, meals, Sports Center

and lifts. AFTER SKI: Bar/lounges in ski village. Swimming pool, hot tub in Sports Center, fee. Two person hot tub in aptmt. SPORTS: X-c ski trail, walking distance. Sports Center: skating, tennis, swimming, racquet ball, weights, exercise classes. Also, snowmobiling, sleigh-riding in valley. CHILDREN: Welcome. Under 12, stay free (nonholiday), under 6, ski free. Child care, fee. SPECIAL: Award-winning design. Passive solar heating. The light through the birch trees.

STONYBROOK RESORT, Luce Hill Rd, Stowe, VT 05672. (802) 253-9701. MAIL: Box 311, Stowe, Vt 05672. RESERVATIONS: same. CREDIT: Cash, check. LOCATION: 3 mi from mountain on access road; secluded. SCALE: 52 aptmts, to be 82. BUILT: 1980-88. PURCHASE: 2BR (1590 sq ft) $205,000 up; 3BR (2170 sq ft) $235,000. up. RENTAL: 2 BR $225 /night; 3BR $ 300/night. Owner decorated to gentle mgmt standard. KITCHEN: Equipped to prepare holiday meal. AMENITIES: W/D, cable TV, touch telephone, fireplace, firewood. SUPPLIES: Grocery store 2.5 mi, liquor store .5 mi. SKIING: 3 mi to ski resort. Public trolley runs between Stowe Village and Mt. Mansfield, past entrance. Car desirable, but not essential. Ski lockers. Rentals, tuning, in village and at mt. AFTER SKI: Stonybrook Community Center inc sauna, jacuzzi, showers, recreation room. Bars/cafes avail along access road and in Stowe Village. SPORTS: X-C skiing, village trail passes Stonybrook, no fee. CHILDREN: Welcome. Game room in Community Center. SPECIAL: The view across the farm toward the mountain.

STOWEFLAKE RESORT, Mountain Road, Stowe, VT, 05672. (802) 253-7355. MAIL: Box 396, Stowe, VT, 06572. RESERVATIONS: (800) 782-9009. CREDIT: VISA, MC, AE, DC. BUILT: 1982-3. SCALE: 24 aptmts. LOCATION: On golf course, 20 acre site. PURCHASE: 2BR (1850 sq ft) $230,000 up. RENTAL: 2 BR $160/night. Daily maid service. Generic furniture package. KITCHEN: Equipped to prepare holiday meal. AMENITIES: W/D in some, color TV, telephone, fireplace, firewood, coffee and filters. SERVICES: Trolley to skiing. SUPPLIES: Grocery 1/2 mi, liquor 2 mi. RESTAURANTS: Winfield's, on-site. Meal plans avail. Catering to apartments avail. SKIING: 4 mi to mountain, free trolley, car desirable. Ski lockers, tuning on-site, tickets at desk. AFTER SKI: Charlie B's, free hors d'ouvres; swimming pool, hot tub in health club; bathtub jacuzzi in aptmts. SPORTS: X-c skiing, swimming, weights, exercise room. CHILDREN: Well-behaved children welcome, teenagers with supervision only. Kids ski and stay free as part of some packages. Child care, fee. Game room. Sleds and tobaggan, fee. SPECIAL: Charlie B's, from 4 pm to midnight.

SUNDAY RIVER CONDOMINIUMS, Sunday River Rd, Bethel, ME 02417. (207) 824-2187. MAIL: Box 450, Bethel, ME 04217. RESERVATIONS: ME (800) 443-1007. US & Canada (800 367-3314. FAX: (207) 824-2111. CREDIT: VISA, MC, AE, DIS. LOCATION: In the ski village, at base of lifts. SCALE: 616 aptmts, to be 688. BUILT: 1978- 89. PURCHASE: 2BR (810 sq ft) $90,000 up; 3BR (1500 sq ft) $198,000 up. RENTAL: 2 BR $180/night; 3BR $240/night. Daily maid service. Generic furniture pkg. KITCHEN: Equipped to provide simple meals. AMENITIES: Cable TV, touch telephone, some fireplaces, firewood. Laundry. Welcome pacs. SUPPLIES: On-site grocery store, liquor store 6 mi. RESTAURANTS: Fall Line, D.W.McKeens. Pizza take-out from grocery. SKIING: Ski-in, ski out most; 100 ft walk, some. Trolley circles ski village. Car not necessary, but desirable. Ski lockers, rentals, tuning on-site, lift tickets charged to room. AFTER-SKI: D.W.McKeens bar. Swimming pool, jacuzzi, saunas. SPORTS: swimming. CHILDREN: Welcome. Under

5, ski free. Game room. Teen activities. Child care, fee. SPECIAL: Advanced lift system, snowmaking. The town of Bethel, 6 mi.

TIMBER CREEK TOWNHOME CONDOMINIUMS, Route 100, West Dover, VT, 05356. (802) 464-2323. MAIL: Box 860, West Dover, VT, 05356. RESERVATIONS: (800) 437-7350. CREDIT: VISA, MC, AE. BUILT: 1984-90. SCALE: 178 aptmts, to be 246 in 1990. LOCATION: Across from the entrance to Mt. Snow. PURCHASE: 2BR (2500 sq ft) $210,000 up. RENTAL: 2 BR $600/weekend, less midweek. Owner decorated to rigorous management standard. KITCHEN: Equipped to prepare holiday meal. AMENITIES: W/D, cable TV, telephone, fireplace, firewood, coffee and filters. SERVICES: Shuttle to skiing. SUPPLIES: Grocery 2 mi, liquor 2 mi. RESTAURANTS: Lounge Deck, on-site. Catering avail. LOCATION: 5 min. to mountain, free shuttle, car not essential. Ski lockers, boot dryers, ski valet. XC rentals on-site. AFTER SKI: Bar/lounge on-site. Health club with swimming pool, hot tub. Bathtub jacuzzi in aptmts. SPORTS: X-c ski center on-site. Swimming, paddle tennis, weights, exercise room, exercise classes, racquet ball. Riding on-site. CHILDREN: Welcome. SPECIAL: Cross country ski center run by expert skier.

VILLAGE WATCH, The Stratton Mountain Resort, Stratton Mountain Rd, Stratton, VT 05155. (802) 297-2200. MAIL: Stratton Mountain Road, Stratton, VT 05155. RESERVATIONS: (800) 843-6867. BUILT: 1985-89. SCALE: 108 aptmts in village, more to come. LOCATION: At base of lifts. PURCHASE: 2BR $250,000 (1200 sq ft). RENTAL: 2BR $ (variable pkgs). Owner decorated, rigorous mgmt standard. KITCHEN: Equipped to prepare holiday meal. AMENITIES: W/D, cable TV, touch telephone in most, fireplace, firewood, toiletries. SUPPLIES: Grocery 1/4 mi, liquor 10 mi. RESTAURANTS: 4 on-site. SKIING: At base of slopes. Car desirable. Good mid-week pkgs. AFTER SKI: Sports Center: swimming pool, hot tub. Lounges, bars in village. SPORTS: X-c skiing, fee. Skating. Sports Center: indoor tennis, racquet ball, sleigh riding, exercise room, classes, weights; fee. CHILDREN: Welcome. Special programs. Child care, fee. SPECIAL: New 12 passenger gondola. The ski village. Indoor tennis. Mulligan's.

WENTWORTH RESORT HOTEL, Rt 16A, Jackson, NH 03846. (603) 383-9700. RESERVATIONS: same. MAIL: Box M, Jackson, NH 03846. CREDIT: VISA,MC,AE. SCALE: 64, to be 92. BUILT: 1880, Wentworth Hotel. 1983-88 aptmts. LOCATION: On village green in historic Vermont town, aptmts on golf course. PURCHASE: 2 BR (1400 sq ft) $175,000 up; 3 BR (2400 sq ft) $260,000 up. RENTAL: 2 BR $200, 3 BR $225; 2 night min. Owner decorated to rigorous mgmt std. KITCHEN: Equipped to prepare holiday meal. AMENITIES: W/D, cable TV, touch telephone, fireplace, firewood. SUPPLIES: On-site grocery, liquor 3 mi. RESTAURANT: The Plum Room. MAP available (B and D). Delivery avail. SKIING: Nearest, 2 mi; best, 10 mi. Car essential. X-C trail crosses site, fee. On-site ski rental and tickets. SPORTS: Skating, sleigh-ride. AFTER SKI: Lounge, bar in hotel. CHILDREN: Welcome. Child care, fee. SPECIAL: Town of Jackson. Jackson Public Library. The view of the mountains.

WHITEFACE RESORT GOLF AND COUNTRY CLUB, Whiteface Inn Rd, Lake Placid, NY 12946. (518) 523-2551. MAIL: Bx 231, Lake Palcid, NY 12946. RESERVATIONS: (518) 523-2551. FAX: (518) 523-2551, x110. CREDIT: VISA, MC, AE, DC, DIS.

BUILT: 1986-92. SCALE: 30 aptmts, to be 90. LOCATION: On Lake Placid, 10 miles from Whiteface. PURCHASE: 2BR $187,000 (1200 sq ft). RENTAL: 2BR $150 and up. Owner decorated, gentle mgmt standard. Daily maid service. KITCHEN: Equipped to prepare simple family meal. AMENITIES: W/D, TV, telephone in most, fireplace, firewood. SERVICES: Airport pickup, fee. Transportation to skiing, fee. SUPPLIES: Grocery 2 mi, liquor 2 mi. RESTAURANT: Whiteface Resort Restaurant on-site. SKIING: 10 miles to Whiteface. Car essential. AFTER SKI: Outdoor swimming pool. Lounge in restaurant. SPORTS: X-c skiing. CHILDREN: Welcome. Older teens with supervision only. SPECIAL: Lake Placid Olympic history. Adirondack culture. The balcony over looking lake.

WINDHAM RIDGE CLUB, Vinning Rd, NY, 12496. (518) 734-5800. MAIL: Box 67, Windham, NY, 12496. RESERVATIONS: (518) 734-5800. CREDIT: VISA, MC. SCALE: 81 aptmts, 180 in 1990. LOCATION: On hilltop, 1.5 miles from mountain. PURCHASE: 2BR (970 sq ft) $140,000 up, 3BR (1650 sq ft) $186,000 up. RENTAL: 2 BR $250/night, 3BR $350/night. Owner decorated, rigorous mgmt standard. KITCHEN: Equipped to prepare holiday meal. AMENITIES: W/D in some, cable TV, touch telephone, fireplace, firewood. SERVICES: Shuttle to skiing. SUPPLIES: Grocery 1/2 mi, liquor 1/2 mi. RESTAURANTS: Fitness Center to contain restaurant. Others in Windham. SKIING: 1.5 mi. to mountain, free shuttle. Car essential. AFTER SKI: Swimming pool, hot tub in Fitness center, fee. SPORTS: Swimming, fee. Tennis, instruction, fee. Exercise room, fee. CHILDREN: Welcome. SPECIAL: All American Sports Tennis Academy and three indoor courts.

WINTERPLACE CONDOMINIUMS, Okemo Ski Resort, RFD #1, Ludlow, VT 05149. (802) 228-4041. MAIL: same. RESERVATIONS: (802) 228-5571. CREDIT: VISA, MC, AE. SCALE: 204 aptmts, to be 246 in 1989. LOCATION: On mountain, chairlift and car access. BUILT: 1985-9. PURCHASE: 2BR (1100 sq ft) $138,000 up. RENTAL: 2 BR $210. Generic furniture package. KITCHEN: Equipped to prepare holiday meal. AMENITIES: W/D, cable TV, telephone, fireplace, firewood, Vermont products package. SUPPLIES: Grocery 1 mi, liquor 1 mi. RESTAURANTS: Clockworks Restaurant in base area. Michael's (tel-228-5622) caters to apartments. SKIING: Aptmts are at top of Mountain Quad chair. Car desirable, but not essential. Ski lockers on-site, rentals and tuning at base. AFTER SKI: Sitting Bull Lounge in base area; swimming pool, hot tub on-site. SPORTS: Swimming. CHILDREN: Welcome. Under 12 stay free, under 6 ski free. Free child care mid-week. Game room in base lodge. Holiday programs. SPECIAL: Winterplace's swimming pool, hot tub. Okemo's enthusiasm for families.

THE WOODS AT KILLINGTON, Killington Rd, Killington, VT 05751. (802) 422-3100. MAIL: RR1 Bx 2210, Killington, VT 05751. RESERVATIONS: (800) 633-0127. FAX: (802) 422-4070. CREDIT: VISA, MC, AE. BUILT: 1985-89. SCALE: 94 aptmts, to be 144. LOCATION: Secluded site off Killington's access road. RENTAL: 2BR $ 233 and up. Owner decorated, gentle mgmt standard. Daily maid service. KITCHEN: Equipped to prepare holiday meal. AMENITIES: W/D, cable TV, touch telephone, fireplace, firewood, loaned bathrobes, toiletries. SERVICES: Transportation to skiing, grocery shopping. SUPPLIES: Grocery 1 mi, liquor 1 mi. RESTAURANTS: Puzant's Restaurant, on-site. Room service avail. Catering avail.

SKIING: Killington 3 mi. Car not essential. AFTER SKI: The Lift lounge on-site. Hot tub, indoor pool. Spa therapy, fee. Jacuzzis in aptmts. SPORTS: Skating, swimming, exercise rooms, classes. CHILDREN: Welcome. Children stay free. SPECIAL: Secluded site. Spa de la Foret.

THE WEST

ASPEN CLUB CONDOMINIUMS, 1421-43 Crystal Lake Rd, Aspen, CO 81611. (303) 920-4000. MAIL: Aspen Club Realty, 520 E. Durant Ave, Aspen, CO 81611. RESERVATIONS: (800) 882-2582. FAX: (303) 920-2000. CREDIT: VISA, MC, AE. SCALE: 20 aptmts. BUILT: 1977. LOCATION: Wooded site, outskirts of town. PURCHASE: 2BR $695,000 (2000 sq ft), 3BR $750,000 (2300 sq ft). RENTAL: 2BR $232 and up, 3BR $318 and up. Owner decorated, rigorous mgmt standard. Daily maid service. KITCHEN: Equipped to prepare holiday meal. AMENITIES: W/D, cable TV, touch telephone, fireplace, firewood, loaned bathrobes, toiletries. SERVICES: Airport pickup. SUPPLIES: Grocery 1/4 mi, liquor 1/4 mi. RESTAURANTS: In Aspen, 1/2 mi. SKIING: 1/2 mi to nearest lift. Car essential. AFTER SKI: Aspen Club: indoor/outdoor swimming pool, hot tub, lounge. SPORTS: X-c skiing. Indoor tennis, racquet ball, exercise room, classes, weights. CHILDREN: Welcome. Game room. Day care. SPECIAL: The Aspen Club sports facilities. Indoor tennis. Convenient to town, secluded from it.

ASPEN PRIVATE HOMES, (various addresses), through Aspen Club Realty, 520 E. Durant Ave, Aspen, CO 81611. (303) 920-4000. MAIL: Aspen Club Realty, 520 E. Durant Ave, Aspen, CO 81611. RESERVATIONS: (800) 882-2582. FAX: (303) 920-2020. CREDIT: VISA, MC, AE. SCALE: 20 or more private homes (listings change). LOCATION: Red Mountain. Central Aspen area. RENTAL: 3BR $218 to $925. Owner decorated, rigorous mgmt standard. Daily maid service. KITCHENS: Equipped to prepare holiday meal. AMENITIES: W/D, cable TV, touch telephone in most, fireplace, firewood, loaned bathrobes, toiletries. SERVICES: Airport pickup. SUPPLIES: Grocery 1/4 mi, liquor 1/4 mi. RESTAURANTS: In Aspen. SKIING: Aspen, Aspen Highlands. Buttermilk, within 6 miles. Snowmass, 12 mi. Car essential. AFTER SKI: Aspen Club sports center: swimming pool and hot tubs. Jacuzzis in most homes. SPORTS: X-c skiing. Aspen Club: tennis, racquet ball, weights, exercise. CHILDREN: Welcome. Day care, fee. Special programs. SPECIAL: Fashionable private homes, comfortable and elegant. Views from Red Mountain.

BEAVERHEAD CONDOMINIUMS, Big Sky, MT. (406) 995-4211. MAIL: Bx 1, Big Sky, MT, 59716. RESERVATIONS: (800) 548-4486. FAX: (406) 995-4860. CREDIT: VISA, MC, AE, DC. BUILT: 1981-89. SCALE: 18 aptmts, to be 58. LOCATION: At base of mountain on ski trail. PURCHASE: 3BR $225,000 (2000 sq ft), 4BR $285,000, (2700 sq ft). RENTAL: 2BR $250, 3BR $330 and up. Owner decorated, rigorous mgmt standard. KITCHEN: Equipped to prepare holiday meal. AMENITIES: W/D in most, cable TV, touch telephone in most, fireplace, firewood. SUPPLIES: Grocery 8 min. walk. liquor, 8 min walk. Transportation supplied. RESTAURANTS: The Huntley Lodge on-site. Furst Place, 5 mi, transportation provided. SKIING: On trail. Car desirable, not essential. On-site ski rentals and tuning. AFTER SKI: Hot tub in each aptmt. Outdoor hot-tub, swimming pool in Huntley Lodge. SPORTS: X-c skiing, fee. Skating. CHILDREN: Welcome. Game room in Huntley Lodge. Holiday programs. SPECIAL: Skiing back to the apartment. The window seat by the fireplace.

BEAVER RUN RESORT, 620 Village Rd, Breckenridge, CO 80424. (303) 453-6000. MAIL: Bx 2115, Breckenridge, CO 80424. RESERVATIONS: (800) 525-2253. FAX: (303) 453-4284. CREDIT: VISA, MC, AE, DC. BUILT: 1979-86. SCALE: 438 aptmts. LOCATION: At base of lifts. RENTAL: 2BR $255 and up. Owner decorated, selection provided by mngt. Daily maid service. KITCHEN: Equipped to prepare holiday meal. AMENITIES: Cable TV, touch telephone, fireplace, firewood, coffee and filters, toiletries. SERVICES: Transportation to skiing, grocery shopping. SUPPLIES: Grocery supplies on-site, grocery 3/4 mi. RESTAURANTS: On-site Spenser's, Coppertop, and G.B.Watson's Deli. SKIING: On trail at base of lift. Car not essential, underground parking. AFTER SKI: 2 swimming pools, 7 outdoor hot tubs. Lounges. Jacuzzis in some aptmts. SPORTS: X-c skiing, fee. Weights, exercise room. Paddle tennis, fee. CHILDREN: Welcome. Game room. Children stay free. Day care, fee. SPECIAL: Outdoor hot tubs on the roof overlooking the slopes.

CHAMONIX AT WOODRUN, 475 Wood Rd, Snowmass Village, CO 81615. (303) 923-3232. MAIL: Bx 6077, Snowmass Village, CO 81615. RESERVATIONS: (800) 635-7480. CREDIT: VISA, MC, AE, DC. BUILT: 1985. SCALE: 28 aptmts. LOCATION: On slope, between two trails. PURCHASE/RENTAL: Rates available on request. Owner decorated, rigorous mgmt standard. Daily maid service. KITCHEN: Equipped to prepare holiday meal. AMENITIES: W/D, cable TV, touch telephone, fireplace, firewood, loaned bathrobes, coffee and filters, toiletries. SERVICES: Airport pickup, transportation to skiing. Grocery shopping, fee. SUPPLIES: Grocery 1/2 mi, liquor 1/2 mi, transportation supplied. RESTAURANTS: In village, within walking distance. SKIING: On trail, ski-down to lifts. Car not necessary. AFTER SKI: Ouytdoor swimming pool, hot tub. Lounge. SPORTS: X-c skiing, skating, fee. Weights, exercise room. CHILDREN: Welcome. Game room, sleds and toboggans, fee. Special programs. Day care, fee. SPECIAL: Elegant apartments with a wonderful view.

THE CHARTER at BEAVER CREEK, 120 Offerson Rd, Beaver Creek, CO 81620. (303) 949-6660. RESERVATIONS: (800) 824-3064. MAIL: Box 5310, Avon, CO 81620. FAX: (303) 949-6709. CREDIT: VISA,MC,AE.DC,CB. SCALE: 156 units. BUILT: 1981-85. LOCATION: In ski village at base of lifts. PURCHASE: 2 BR (1200 sq ft) $226,000 up; 3 BR (1800 sq ft) $390,000 up. RENTAL: 2 BR $370. Skier packages available. Owner decorated to gentle mgmt std. Daily maid service. KITCHEN: Equipped to prepare holiday meal. AMENITIES: W/D, cable TV, touch telephone, fireplace, firewood. SUPPLIES: Small grocery on-site. Grocery and liquor stores, 3 mi. Car useful, not essential. Underground parking. RESTAURANTS: on site: The Terrace, and The First Season. SKIING: 300 yds to lift. Ski lockers, rental, tuning and tickets on site. SPORTS: On-site health club, swimming pool, hot tub, weights. AFTER SKI: Forum Lounge, fireplace. CHILDREN: Welcome. Under 12 stay free. SPECIAL: The elegant European swimming pool.

CIMARRON LODGE, Coonskin Base Area, Telluride, CO. (303) 728-3803. MAIL: Telluride Accommodations, Bx 756, Telluride, CO 81435. RESERVATIONS: (800) 233-9292. CREDIT: VISA, MC, AE, CHOICE. SCALE: 40 aptmts. BUILT: 1983. LOCATION: At base of Coonskin Lift. PURCHASE:

2BR $160,000 (1100 sq ft). RENTAL: 2BR $240p. Renovated inside and out 1987-88. Furnished by mgmt, owner additions; gentle mgmt standard. Daily maid service. KITCHEN: Equipped to prepare family meal. AMENITIES: W/D in most, cable TV, touch telephone, welcome pac. SERVICES: Airport pickup, fee. Grocery shopping, fee. SUPPLIES: Grocery, 2 blocks, liquor 6 blocks, delivery avail. RESTAURANTS: In complex, others within walking distance. SKIING: Ski-in and out, at base of Coonskin Lift. On-site ski tuning and rentals. Ticket office in building. Car unnecessary after arrival. Underground pkg. AFTER SKI: Pub on-site. Group hot tub and changing rooms. SPORTS: Riding and sleigh-riding, next door. CHILDREN: Welcome. Child care nearby, fee. Children's activities on mountain. SPECIAL: The view of the mountain from Cimarron Lodge. The town of Telluride.

CRESTED MOUNTAIN VILLAGE and PLAZA, 21 Emmons Rd, Crested Butte, CO 81224. (303) 349-7555. MAIL: Resort Management Group, Bx 99, Crested Butte, CO 81224. RESERVATIONS: (800) 282-2013. CREDIT: VISA, MC, AE, DC, DIS. SCALE: 128 apartments, to be 188. BUILT: 1979, still adding. LOCATION: At base of slopes. RENTAL: 2BR $230. Mgmt decorated, with owner contributions. Daily maid service. KITCHEN: Equipped to prepare holiday meal. AMENITIES: W/D, cable TV, touch telephone, fireplace, firewood, coffee and filters, toiletries. SERVICES: Airport pickup, grocery shopping, fee. SUPPLIES: Grocery 100 yards, liquor 100 yards. RESTAURANTS: Jeremiah's, Tin Cup Cafe and Bakery, Black Bear, in village. SKIING: At base of slopes. Car not necessary. AFTER SKI: Swimming pool, hot tubs, lounge. Some apartments with hot tubs or jacuzzis. SPORTS: X-c skiing, fee. Swimming, weights. CHILDREN: Welcome. Special programs. Day care, fee. SPECIAL: Proximity to slopes, comfortable apartments, uncrowded resort.

DELTA MOUNTAIN INN, 4050 Whistler Way, Whistler, BC VON 1B0 Canada. (604) 932-1982. MAIL: Bx 550, Whistler, BC VON 1B0 RESERVATIONS: (604) 932-1982, x313. TELEX: 04 508318. FAX: (604) 932-2405. CREDIT: VISA, MC, AE, DC, CB. SCALE: 300 aptmts. BUILT: 1982-88. LOCATION: At base of slopes. RENTAL: 1BR $225 CDN. Mgmt decorated. Daily maid service. KITCHEN: Equipped to prepare holiday meal. AMENITIES: W/Ds in building, cable TV, touch telephone, fireplace, firewood, loaned bathrobes, toiletries. SUPPLIES: Grocery, liquor within walking distance. RESTAURANT: Twigs Restaurant in building, take-out and room service avail. SKIING: Whistler and Blackcomb within few yards. Car undesirable, underground pkg. AFTER SKI: Outdoor pool, indoor and out door hot tubs. Twigs Lounge. SPORTS: Indoor tennis, 2 courts. Exercise machines. X-c skiing, fee. CHILDREN: Welcome. Game room, holiday programs. Children stay free. SPECIAL: A resort itself within Whistler/Blackcomb's resort.

GRAND TARGHEE RESORT, Alta, WY, (307) 353-2304. MAIL: Grand Targhee Resort, Bx SKI, Alta, WY 83422. RESERVATIONS: (800) 443-8146. FAX: (307) 353-8148. CREDIT: VISA, MC, AE. SCALE: 32 aptmts. LOCATION: In ski village at base of slopes. RENTAL: 2BR $183. Mgmt decorated in recent renovation. Daily maid service. KITCHEN: Equipped to prepare family meal. AMENITIES: W/D in adjacent building, TV, touch telephone, fireplace, firewood, toiletries. SERVICES: Airport pickup, fee. Grocery shopping, fee. SUPPLIES: General store on-site. Grocery 12 mi, liquor 12 mi. RESTAURANTS: Skati's. Cafeteria and snack bar. SKIING: At base of mountain. Car not essential. AFTER SKI: Outdoor swimming pool, indoor hot tub. Trap Bar. SPORTS: X-c skiing. Instruction in both nordic and ski touring. Snowcat skiing. CHILDREN: Affirmatively welcome. Child care days and evening. Family program every

night. SPECIAL: Grand Targhee powder. The view from the new Sioux Lodge. Family-focused resort.

GRANLIBAKKEN SKI AND RACQUET RESORT, Granlibakken Rd, Tahoe City, CA 95730. (916) 583-4242. MAIL: Bx 6329, Tahoe City, CA 95730. RESERVATIONS: (800) 543-3221 (CA only), (916) 583-4242. FAX: (916) 583-7461. CREDIT: VISA, MC, AE, DC, CB, DIS. SCALE: 76 aptmts. BUILT: 1976. LOCATION: 1 mi from Lake Tahoe. RENTAL: 2BR $ 177 and up. Owner decorated, gentle mgmt standard. Daily maid service. KITCHEN: Equipped to prepare holiday meal. AMENITIES: W/D in laundry room, cable TV, touch telephone in most, fireplace in most, toiletries. SERVICES: Airport pickup, fee. Transportation to skiing. SUPPLIES: Grocery, 1 mi, liquor 1 mi. RESTAURANT: Full bkft included. SKIING: Squaw Valley, 6 mi, Alpine Meadows, 6 mi. Transportation provided. Car desirable. AFTER SKI: Group hot tub. SPORTS: X-c skiing. Downhill skiing and instruction on-site. CHILDREN: Welcome in family groups. SPECIAL: Secluded site in Lake Tahoe area. Breakfast.

HEARTHSTONE LODGE, 4211 Sunshine Pl, Whistler, BC, Canada. (604) 932-4161. MAIL: Whistler Chalets, 206-1650 Duranleau, Granville Island, Vancouver, BC V6H 3S4, Canada. RESERVATIONS: (604)669-5353. TELEX: 0451208, answer back WSLR/WSLR. FAX: (604) 932-2027. CREDIT: VISA, MC, AE. SCALE: 21 aptmts. BUILT: 1980. LOCATION: Overlooking Village Square, in Whistler Village at base of slopes. PURCHASE: 2BR $178,000 CDN (1350 sq ft). RENTAL: 2BR $190 CDN, and up. Furniture designed by architect. Daily maid service. KITCHEN: Equipped to prepare holiday meal. AMENITIES: W/D in building, cable TV, touch telephone in most, fireplace, firewood, coffee and filters, toiletries, welcome pacs. SUPPLIES: Grocery and liquor store in building. RESTAURANT: Peter's Underground Restaurant in building. Others within walking distance. SKIING: Whistler and Blackcomb lifts, 75 yards. Ski tuning in building. Car undesirable, underground pkg. AFTER SKI: Health club in adjoining building, swimming pool, hot tubs. Pub in building. SPORTS: X-c skiing. Health Club: racquet sports, swimming, exercise machines and classes. CHILDREN: Welcome. Under 6 stay free and ski free. SPECIAL: View through angled skylights of Blackcomb ski trails and Whistler's rooftops.

IRON HORSE RESORT, 257 Winter Park Dr, Winter Park, CO 80482. (303) 726-8851. MAIL: Bx 1286, Winter Park, CO 80482. RESERVATIONS: (800) 621-8190. FAX: (303) 726-8851 x 6023. CREDIT: VISA; MC, AE. BUILT: 1982-85. SCALE: 126 aptmts. LOCATION: Between Winter Park and Mary Jane ski areas, ski-in, ski-out. RENTAL: 2BR $200 (850 sq ft). Packages avail. Aptmts furnished by mgmt, with owners. Daily maid service. KITCHEN: Equipped to prepare holiday meal. AMENITIES: W/D in most, cable TV, touch telephone, fireplace, firewood, coffee and filters, toiletries. SERVICES: Airport pickup and transportation to grocery. SUPPLIES: Small grocery on-site. Grocery 4 mi, liquor 2 mi, transportation supplied. RESTAURANTS: The Rails. Take-out avail. SKIING: On trail, Winter Park's Zephyr nearest lift. Car not essential, underground pkg. AFTER SKI: 4 outdoor hot tubs. In door/outdoor pool. Rails' lounge. SPORTS: X-c skiing, skating available locally. Weights, exercise room. CHILDREN: Welcome. Teenagers with supervision. Game room. Children ski and stay free. SPECIAL: Iron Horse Resort adjoins National Forest and Winter Park ski area.

KEYSTONE RESORT, Keystone, CO 80435. (303) 468-2316. MAIL: Bx 38 Keystone, CO, 80435. RESERVATIONS: (800) 222-0188. CREDIT: VISA, MC, AE, DC. SCALE: 27 aptmts. BUILT: 1982. LOCATION: At base of slopes. PURCHASE: 2BR $260,000 (1500 sq ft). RENTAL: $ variable, pkgs avail. Owner decorated, rigorous mgmt standard. KITCHEN: Equipped to prepare holiday meal. AMENITIES: W/D, cable TV, touch telephone, fireplace, firewood, toiletries. SERVICES: Airport pickup, fee. Grocery shopping. SUPPLIES: Grocery, 1 mi, liquor 1/4 mi, transportation supplied. RESTAURANTS: Within walking distance. SKIING: At base of slope. Car desirable, not essential. Public transportation to other resorts. AFTER SKI: Group hot tubs in aptmts. Pubs within walking distance. SPORTS: X-c skiing, fee. Skating, fee. CHILDREN: Welcome. Under 12 stay free. Child care, fee. SPECIAL: Medieval castle, onslope. Night skiing at Keystone.

LAKELAND VILLAGE BEACH AND SKI RESORT, South Lake Tahoe, CA 95705 (916) 541-7711. MAIL: Bx 705002, south Lake Tahoe, CA 95705-7502. RESERVATIONS: (800) 822-5969. BUILT: late'70s. SCALE: 180 aptmts. LOCATION: On 1000 ftbeach, south shore of Lake Tahoe. RENTAL: 2BR $170. Owner decorated, rigorous mgmt standard. KITCHEN: Equipped to prepare family meal. AMENITIES: Cable TV, touch telephone in most, fireplace, firewood, toiletries. SUPPLIES: Grocery 1/2 mi, liquor 1/2 mi. RESTAURANTS: Shuttle to Nevada casinos. SKIING: 1 mi. Car essential. AFTER SKI: 2 Swimming pools, hot tub. Nevada casinos. SPORTS: X-c skiing. Swimming. CHILDREN: Welcome. SPECIAL: Lake Tahoe.

THE LODGE AT STEAMBOAT, 2700 Village Dr, Steamboat Springs, CO 80477. (303) 879-6000. MAIL: Steamboat Resorts, Bx 2995, Steamboat Springs, CO 80477. RESERVATIONS: (800) 525-5502. FAX: (303) 879-8060. CREDIT: VISA, MC, AE. BUILT: 1979. SCALE: 113 aptmts. LOCATION: At base of slopes. RENTAL: 2BR $ and up. Owner decorated, rigorous mgmt standard. Daily maid service. KITCHEN: Equipped to prepare holiday meal. Staples left for use. AMENITIES: W/D in building, cable TV, touch telephone, fireplace, firewood, coffee and filters. SERVICES: Transportation to skiing. SUPPLIES: Grocery 1 mi, liquor 50 yards, transportation supplied. RESTAURANTS: AM coffee and donuts. Restaurants near-by. SKIING: Gondola adjacent to aptmt. Car not necessary. AFTER SKI: 2 outdoor, 1 indoor hot tubs. Lounge. SPORTS: X-c skiing, skating, swimming in village. CHILDREN: Welcome. Stay free and ski free with certain pkgs. SPECIAL: Convenient, comfortable apartments. Kids ski, stay free. Good choice for families.

LODGE TOWER IN VAIL VILLAGE, 200 Vail Rd, Vail CO 81657. (303) 476-9530. MAIL: 200 Vail Rd, Vail, CO 81657. RESERVATIONS: (800) 654-2517. FAX: (303) 476-4093. CREDIT: VISA, MC, AE, CB. BUILT: 1973. SCALE: 42 aptmts. LOCATION: Center of Vail, at base of mountain. PURCHASE: 2BR $365,000 (1205 sq ft), 3BR $ 500,000 (1600 sq ft). RENTAL: 2BR $270, 3BR $ 360 and up. Owner decorated, rigorous mgmt standard. Daily maid service. KITCHEN: Equipped to prepare holiday meal. AMENITIES: Cable TV, touch telephone, fireplace, firewood, toiletries. SUPPLIES: Grocery 1 block; liquor 1 block. RESTAURANTS: Continental bkft included. Restaurants within walking distance. SKIING: 1 block to Vista Bahn lift. Car undesirable. AFTER SKI: Hot tub. Lounge. SPORTS: X-c skiing and skating available in village. CHILDREN: Welcome. 12 and under stay free. SPECIAL: Seven story building with views of village and mountain.

NORTHSTAR-AT-TAHOE, at CA Highway 267 and Northstar Dr, Truckee, CA 95724. (916) 587-0200. MAIL: Northstar-at-Tahoe, Bx 124, Truckee, CA 95724. RESERVATIONS: (800) 533-6787. FAX: (916) 587-0214. CREDIT: VISA, MC, AE, DIS. SCALE: 654 aptmts, to be 3,100. BUILT: 1972-89, still adding. LOCATION: In 6,000 acre property, inc ski

area. RENTAL: 2BR $155, 3BR $178 and up. Owner decorated, rigorous mgmt standard. KITCHEN: Equipped to prepare holiday meal. AMENITIES: W/D in most, cable TV, touch telephone in most, fireplace in most, firewood. SERVICES: Airport pickup with notice. SUPPLIES: Grocery 8 mi, liquor 8 mi, convenience store on-site. RESTAURANTS: Schaffer's Mill, Basque Club, Pedro's. SKIING: Gondola to ski area from Village Plaza. Ski Trail condos ski-back. Others by shuttle 1 mi. Car desirable. AFTER SKI: Hot tubs in recreation center. SPORTS: Weights and exercise room; x-c skiing, fee. CHILDREN: Welcome. SPECIAL: Between Lake Tahoe and Truckee. Navada casino nightlife.

MOTHERLODE CONDOMINIUMS, Park Ave, corner of Main St, Park City, UT. (801)649-3800. MAIL: Le Concierge Property Management, Bx 536, Park City, UT 84060. RESERVATIONS: (800) 824-1672. CREDIT: VISA, MC, AE. SCALE: 15 aptmts. BUILT: 1985. LOCATION: In Old Town, close to Town Lift. PURCHASE: 2BR $100,000 (1100 sq ft). RENTAL: 2BR $225. Owner decorated, professional mgmt std. KITCHEN: Equipped to prepare holiday meal. AMENITIES: W/D in some, cable TV, touch telephone in most, fireplace, firewood. SERVICES: Grocery shopping, fee. SUPPLIES: Grocery 1 mi, liquor 1 block. RESTAURANTS: Within walking distance. SKIING: Town Lift 50 yards, ski back. Car not essential. AFTER SKI: Group outdoor hot tub. Pubs within walking distance. SPORTS: X-c skiing, skating, indoor tennis availailable in town. CHILDREN: Welcome. SPECIAL: Proximity to Town Lift and Old Town nightlife.

PARK PLAZA AT BEAVER CREEK, 46 Avondale Lane, Beaver Creek, CO 61620. (303) 845-7700. MAIL: Bx 36, Beaver Creek, CO 81620. RESERVATIONS: (303) 845-7700. FAX: (303) 845-7700. CREDIT: VISA, MC, AE. SCALE: 36 apartments. BUILT: 1985. LOCATION: At base of slopes. RENTAL: 2BR $ 350 and up. Furniture packages provided. Daily maid service. KITCHEN: Equipped to prepare holiday meal. AMENITIES: W/D, cable TV, touch telephone, fireplace, firewood, loaned bathrobes, coffee and filters, toiletries. SERVICES: Transportation to Vail skiing, grocery shopping, valet parking. SUPPLIES: Grocery 1 block, liquor 1 block. RESTAURANTS: Continental bkft. SKIING: At base of Beaver Creek. Car desirable, not essential. AFTER SKI: Swimming pool and group hot tub. SPORTS: X-c skiing. Skating. CHILDREN: Welcome. Special programs. Children's ski playground on slope. SPECIAL: Luxuriously decorated, elegant residence.

RACQUET CLUB CONDOMINIUMS, Racquet Club Dr, Park City, UT 84068. (801) 649-9598. MAIL: Jupiter Property Management, Bx 680128, Park City, UT 84068. RESERVATIONS: (800) 453-5789. CREDIT: VISA, MC, AE. BUILT: 1977-9. SCALE: 180 aptmts. LOCATION: Beside golf course, 1 1/2 mi from Park City Ski Area. PURCHASE: 2BR $89,000 (1800 sq ft). RENTAL: 2BR $150 and up. Decorated from pkg provided by mgmt; redecorated by owners to taste, gentle mgmt standard. KITCHEN: Equipped to prepare family meals. AMENITIES: W/D in most, cable TV, touch telephone in most, fireplace, firewood. SUPPLIES: Grocery 1 1/2 mi, liquor 1 1/2 mi. RESTAURANT: Sneakers Restaurant in Racquet Club, lunch and dinner. SKIING: 1 1/2 mi to Park City and to Park West. Free city shuttle. Car not essential. AFTER SKI: Hot tub, sauna, outdoor pool in Racquet Club, fee. Lounge in Sneakers Restaurant. SPORTS: X-c skiing. Tennis, racquet ball, exercise classes in Racquet Club, fee. CHILDREN: Welcome. Older teens with supervision. Child care available, fee. SPECIAL: Tennis in the Racquet Club. Cross country skiing by moonlight.

THE RESORT CENTER LODGE AND INN, 1415 Lowell Ave, Park City, UT 84060. (801) 649-0800. MAIL: The Resort Center, Bx 3449, Park City, UT 84060. RESERVATIONS: (800) 824-5331. CREDIT: VISA, MC, AE. SCALE: 91 aptmts, 36 shops and restaurants, meeting rooms, health center, around skiers' plaza. BUILT: 1984. LOCATION: At base of Park City ski slopes. RENTAL: 2BR $265. Mngmt furnished, owner additions. Daily maid service. KITCHEN: Equipped to prepare family meal. AMENITIES: W/D on each floor, TV, touch telephone in most, gas fireplace, coffee and filters, toiletries. SUPPLIES: Grocery within The Resort Center. Liquor store 1 mi. RESTAURANTS: The Columbine Restaurant. Four others in plaza area. SKIING: On-slope. Car undesirable. Underground parking. AFTER SKI: Indoor/outdor pool, hot tubs, sauna, steam room. Steeps (pub). SPORTS: On-site skating rink. Fitness Center, weight room, swimming. CHILDREN: Welcome. Child care, fee. On-site ski school. SPECIAL: A resort with the resort.

RIDGEPOINT, Deer Valley, Park City, UT 84068. (801) 649-9598. MAIL: Jupiter Property Mgmt, Bx 680128, Park City, UT 84068. RESERVATIONS: (800) 453-5789. CREDIT: VISA, MC, AE. SCALE: 36 apartments. BUILT: 1985. LOCATION: In Silver Lake area of Deer Valley. PURCHASE: 3BR $219,000 (2800 sq ft). RENTAL: 3BR $ 285 and up. Owner decorated. KITCHEN: Equipped to prepare holiday meal. AMENITIES: W/D, cable TV, fireplace, firewood, coffee and filters. SUPPLIES: Grocery, 3 mi, liquor 3 mi. RESTAURANTS: Cafe Mariposa, in ski village. SKIING: Ski-out by skiers' bridge. Car desirable. AFTER SKI: Group outdoor hot tub. CHILDREN: Welcome. SPECIAL: Comfortable, large. The view.

RIVER MOUNTAIN LODGE, 100 South Park Street, Breckenridge, CO 80424. (303) 453-4711. MAIL: Bx 7188, Breckenridge, CO 80424. RESERVATIONS: (800) 325-2342. CREDIT: VISA, MC, AE, DIS. BUILT: 1986. SCALE: 55 aptmts, to be 162. LOCATION: In center of town, at bottom of ski-back trail. RENTAL: 2BR $190 and up (1250 sq ft). Owner decorated, selection provided by mgmt. Daily maid service. KITCHEN: Equipped to prepare holiday meal. AMENITIES: W/D, cable TV, touch telephone, fireplace, firewood, toiletries. SUPPLIES: Grocery next door, liquor next door. RESTAURANTS: Continental bkft on-site. Restaurants within walking distance. SKIING: Free shuttle every 10 min to lift, 1/2 mi. Car not necessary; underground pkg provided. AFTER SKI: Outdoor hot tub, indoor hot tub. Steamroom, sauna. Lounge, entertainment. SPORTS: Weights, exercise room. CHILDREN: Welcome. 12 and under stay free. SPECIAL: The lobby/lounge's Western-elegant decor and friendly spirit.

SADDLE CONDOMINIUMS, Saddle View Way, Park City, UT 84060. 801 649-6368. MAIL: park City Resort Lodging, 3770 N. Highway 224, Park City, UT 84060. RESERVATIONS: (800) 545-SNOW. CREDIT: VISA, MC, AE. SCALE: 16 apartments. BUILT: 1981. LOCATION: In cul-de-sac, bewteen Park City and Park West resorts. PURCHASE: 3BR $200,000 (2,000 sq ft). RENTAL: 3BR $210. Owner decorated, rigorous mgmt standard. KITCHEN: Equipped to prepare holiday meal. Staples left for use. AMENITIES: W/D in some, cable TV in some, fireplace, firewood, coffee filters. SERVICES: Airport pickup, transportation to skiing, fee. Grocery shopping, fee. SUPPLIES: Grocery 1 mi, liquor 1 mi. RESTAURANTS: In Park City's Old Town, Deer Valley and Park City. Free shuttle bus. SKIING: 1 1/2 mi to either Park City and Park West. 4 mi to Deer Valley. Free shuttle. Car not essential. AFTER SKI: Group hot tub and sauna in each aptmt. CHILDREN: Welcome. SPECIAL: Privacy. Secluded site, convenient to 2 ski areas.

SILVER KING HOTEL, 1485 Empire Ave, Park City, UT 84060. (801) 649-5500. MAIL: Bx 2818, Park City, Ut 84060. RESERVATIONS: (800) 331-8652. FAX: (801) 649-6647. CREDIT: VISA, MC, AE, CB, CHOICE. SCALE: 64 apartments. BUILT: 1984. LOCATION: At base of slopes. RENTAL: 2BR $295 and up. Owner decorated from mgmt pkg. Daily maid service. KITCHEN: Equipped to prepare holiday meal. AMENITIES: W/D, cable TV, touch telephone, fireplace, firewood, coffee and filters, toiletries. SERVICES: Front desk, rentals, lift tickets at deck. SUPPLIES: Grocery 1 block, liquor 2 blocks. RESTAURANTS: Breakfast room on-site. Restaurants within walking distance. SKIING: Park City, across street; Park West, 2 mi; Deer Valley 3 mi. Free shuttle. Car not necessary. AFTER SKI: Indoor-outdoor pool. Group hot tub. Hot tub in some units. SPORTS: Swimming on site, others nearby. CHILDREN: Welcome, well behaved preferred. SPECIAL: 93 steps to nearest lift.

SNOWCREEK RESORT, 85 Old Mammoth Road, Mammoth Lakes, CA 93546. (916) 934-6861. MAIL: Bx 657, Mammoth lakes, CA 93546. RESERVATIONS: (800) 544-6007. CREDIT: VISA, MC. SCALE: 460 apmts/homes. BUILT: 1979-89. LOCATION: Meadow at base of mountain range PURCHASE: 2BR $122,000, 3BR $193,000 up. RENTAL: 2BR $120, 3BR $150 and up. Owner decorated, rigorous mgmt standard. KITCHEN: Equipped to prepare holiday meal. AMENITIES: W/D in some, cable TV, telephone in most, fireplace, firewood. SERVICES: Transportation to skiing. SUPPLIES: Grocery 2 mi, liquor 2 mi. RESTAURANTS: In Mammoth Lakes, 2 mi. SKIING: Mammoth Mountain, 2 mi. Car desirable. AFTER SKI: Hot tub and swimming pool in Sports Center, fee. SPORTS: Racquetball, weights and exercise room, exercise classes in Sports Center, fee. X-c skiing, fee. CHILDREN: Welcome. SPECIAL: California sunshine. The Sports Center. The view.

SPRING CREEK RANCH, Jackson, WY. (307) 733-8833. MAIL: Bx 3154, Jackson WY 83001. RESERVATIONS: (800) 443-6139. FAX: (307) 733-9678. CREDIT: VISA, MC, AE. SCALE: 91 aptmts, to be 300. BUILT: 1982-89 and adding. LOCATION: On mesa outside town of Jackson. PURCHASE: 2BR $90,000 1/4 share (2000 sq ft). RENTAL: 2BR $180 and up. Owner decorated, rigorous mgmt standard. Daily maid service. KITCHEN: Equipped to prepare holiday meal. AMENITIES: W/D in most, cable TV, touch telephone, fireplace, firewood, loaned bathrobes, coffee and filters, toiletries. SERVICES: Airport pickup, transportation to skiing. Grocery shopping, fee. SUPPLIES: Grocery 4 mi, liquor 4 mi, transportation supplied. RESTAURANT: The Granery. Rooms service avail. SKIING: 12 miles to Jackson Hole. Car desirable, not essential. AFTER SKI: The Granery lounge. Outdoor hot tub next to waterfall. SPORTS: X-c skiing. Skating. CHILDREN: Welcome. SPECIAL: The Granery at sunset.

SQUAW VALLEY LODGE, 210 Squaw Peak Rd, Olympic Valley, CA 95730. (916) 583-5500. MAIL: Bx 2665, Olympic Valley, CA 95730. RESERVATIONS: (800) 992-9920, in Ca. (800) 992-9970. CREDIT: VISA, MC, AE. SCALE: 95 aptmts, to be 295. BUILT: 1986-89, still adding. LOCATION: At base of Squaw Valley lifts. PURCHASE: 1BR $150,00 (700 sq ft). RENTAL: 1BR $165 and up. Furniture designed for aptmts. Daily maid service. KITCHEN: Equipped to prepare simple family meal. AMENITIES: Cable TV, touch telephone, coffee and filters, toiletries. SERVICES: Valet parking. SUPPLIES: Grocery 3 mi, liquor 4 mi. RESTAURANT: Breakfast buffet in lobby. Car desirable for dining out. SKIING: Next to tram building. AFTER SKI: Common room. Health club, group hot tub, swimming pool. CHILDREN: Welcome,

well-behaved preferred. SPECIAL: Attractive, efficient apartments. Tram rises over the swimming pool.

STAG LODGE AT DEER VALLEY, 8200 Royal St, Park City, UT 84060. (801) 649-7444. MAIL: Deer Valley Lodging, Bx 3000, Park City, UT 84060. RESERVATIONS: (800) 453-3833. CREDIT: VISA, MC, AE. SCALE: 35 apartments, to be 52. BUILT: 1986-89 and adding. LOCATION: On ridge beside ski trail. PURCHASE: 3BR $675,000 (2400 sq ft). RENTAL: 3BR $ 725 and up. Owner decorated. Daily maid service. KITCHEN: Equipped to prepare holiday meal. AMENITIES: W/D, cable TV, touch telephone, fireplace, firewood, coffee and filters, toiletries. SERVICES: Airport pickup, fee. Grocery shopping, fee. SUPPLIES: Grocery 3 mi, liquor 3 mi. RESTAURANTS: Phillipe's, on-site. Meal plan. SKIING: On Deer Valley ski trail. Park City 3 mi. Car desirable. AFTER SKI: Group outdoor hot tub. Lounge. Hot tubs in most aptmts. CHILDREN: Welcome. SPECIAL: The view, the location, the decor, the architecture. Phillipe's.

ST. BERNARD CONDOMINIUM, Taos Ski Valley, NM 87525. (505) 776-8506. RESERVATIONS: same. MAIL: same. CREDIT: VISA,MC,AE. SCALE: 1988 18 units. BUILT: 1982 (18 units). LOCATION: In ski village at base of slopes. PURCHASE: 2 BR (1250 sq ft) $275,000 up; 3 BR (1630 sq ft) $320,000 up. RENTAL: 2 BR $275 (1-4 people), $290 (5-6). Daily maid service. Furniture package provided with purchase. KITCHEN: Equipped to prepare holiday meal. AMENITIES: Color TV, telephone, fireplace, firewood provided. SUPPLIES: Grocery and liquor within village. RESTAURANT: Hotel St. Bernard. MAP available (D only). SKIING: 10 min. walk to lift; ski lockers in Hotel St. Bernard, base of lift. Car not essential, carport adjoins aptmt. Ski rental, tuning and tickets within village. AFTER SKI: Bar and hot tub in Hotel St. Bernard. Taos 1/2 hr. drive. CHILDREN: Welcome. SPECIAL: The view of Al's run. Ski School. Taos.

SUGARPLUM TOWNHOUSES, Snowbird By-Pass Road, Alta, UT. (801) 742-3880. MAIL: Canyon Services, Bx 25, Snowbird, UT 84092. RESERVATIONS: (801) 943-1842. CREDIT: VISA, MC, AE. SCALE: 30 aptmts, to be 46. BUILT: 1985-88 AND ADDING. LOCATION: On ski trail, above Snowbird Resort. PURCHASE: 2BR $235,000 (1450 sq ft), 3BR $500,000 (3,000 sq ft). RENTAL: 2BR $ 275, 3BR $325. Owner decorated, lavishly. KITCHEN: Equipped to prepare holiday meal. Staples left for use. AMENITIES: W/D, cable TV, touch telephone, fireplace, firewood. SERVICES: Airport pickup, fee; grocery shopping, fee. SUPPLIES: Grocery 1/2 mi, liquor 1/2 mi. RESTAURANTS: Five in Snowbird Resort. Alta Lodge, 1/2 mi, shuttle avail. SKIING: On Snowbird trail. Car desirable. AFTER SKI: Outdoor hot-tub, sauna. SPORTS: X-c skiing. CHILDREN: Welcome, well-behaved preferred. SPECIAL: Little Cottonwood Canyon. The view.

VILLAGE INN PLAZA, 100 E. Meadow Dr, Vail, CO 81657. (303) 476-5622. MAIL: 100 E. Meadow Dr, Vail, CO 81657. RESERVATIONS: (800) 445-4014. CREDIT: VISA, MC, AE, DC, CB. SCALE: 39 apartments. BUILT: 1978-88. LOCATION: Center of Vail Village. PURCHASE: 2BR $225,000 (1100 sq ft) and up. RENTAL: 2BR $250 and up. Owner decorated, gentle mgmt standard. Daily maid service. KITCHEN: Equipped to prepare holiday meal. AMENITIES: W/D, cable TV, touch telephone, fireplace, firewood, coffee and filters, toiletries. SERVICES: Airport pickup, grocery shopping, fee. SUPPLIES: Grocery 1 block, liquor 1 block. Some supplies on-site. RESTAURANTS: Ambrosia, Alpenrose, Pancake House, on-site. SKIING: 2 block

walk. Car undesirable. AFTER SKI: Outdoor pool, some aptmts with jacuzzis. Lounge. SPORTS: Available in Vail; X-c skiing, skating, swimming, riding, snowmobiling, sleigh-riding available in village. CHILDREN: Welcome. SPECIAL: Elegant apartments with hotel services in the heart of Vail.

VAIL RACQUET CLUB CONDOMINIUMS, 4690 Racquet Club Dr, Vail, CO 81657. (303) 476-4840. MAIL: Bx 1437, Vail, CO 81657. RESERVATIONS: (303) 476-4840. CREDIT: VISA, MC, AE, DC. BUILT: 1975-82. SCALE: 306 apartments. LOCATION: Quiet residential area beside river, 4 mi from center of Vail village. PURCHASE: 2BR $115,000 (864 sq ft), 3BR $178,000 (1600 sq ft). RENTAL: 2BR $180; 3BR $225 and up. Owner decorated, rigorous mgmt standard. KITCHEN: Equipped to prepare holiday meal. AMENITIES: W/D on premises, cable TV, touch telephone in most, fireplace, firewood. SUPPLIES: Grocery 1 mi, liquor 1 mi. Will deliver, fee. RESTAURANT: Vail Racquet Club Restaurant, dinner only. Catering available. SKIING: 4 mi to Vail. Free shuttle. Car not necessary. AFTER SKI: Indoor swimming pool, indoor and outdoor hot tubs. SPORTS: X-c skiing. Health Club: tennis, racquet ball, paddle tennis, hand ball, squash, weights, exercise room, exercise classes, trainers; fee. CHILDREN: Welcome. 12 and under stay free. SPECIAL: The health club and the restaurant.

INDEX